Lucinda
A Memoir of a Songwriter's Journey

"Music is not just a job, it is my life"

-Lucinda Williams-

By ROMAN MANRIQUEZ

Copyright © 2023 by ROMAN MANRIQUEZ
All rights reserved.

The content of this book may not be reproduced, duplicated, or transmitted without the author's or publisher's express written permission. Under no circumstances will the publisher or author be held liable or legally responsible for any damages, reparation, or monetary loss caused by the information contained in this book, whether directly or indirectly.

Legal Notice:

This publication is copyrighted. It is strictly for personal use only. You may not change, distribute, sell, use, quote, or paraphrase any part of this book without the author's or publisher's permission.

Disclaimer Notice:

Please keep in mind that the information in this document is only for educational and entertainment purposes. Every effort has been made to present accurate, up-to-date, reliable, and comprehensive information. There are no express or implied warranties. Readers understand that the author is not providing legal, financial, medical, or professional advice. This book's content was compiled from a variety of sources. Please seek the advice of a licensed professional before attempting any of the techniques described in this book. By reading this document, the reader agrees that the author is not liable for any direct or indirect losses incurred as a result of using the information contained within this document, including, but not limited to, errors, omissions, or inaccuracies.

TABLE OF CONTENTS

Introduction

Chapter 1
Chapter 2
Chapter 3
Chapter 4
Chapter 5
Chapter 6
Chapter 7
Chapter 8
Chapter 9
Chapter 10
Chapter 11
Chapter 12
Chapter 13
Chapter 14
Chapter 15
Chapter 16
Chapter 17
Chapter 18
Chapter 19
Chapter 20
Chapter 21
Chapter 22
Chapter 23
Chapter 24

Epilogue

Introduction

Lucinda Williams is a well-known singer, songwriter, and musician in the genres of rock, folk, and country music. She is a seventeen-time Grammy Award nominee and three-time winner, as well as a twelve-time Americana Award candidate and winner. Williams was voted "America's best songwriter" by Time and one of the "100 Greatest Songwriters of All Time" by Rolling Stone.

Chapter 1

My father would drink gin and tonics in the summer. "Honey, can you go make me a drink?" he used to say when I was a youngster. I knew how to pour gin into a shot glass and then into a cocktail glass with ice, followed by tonic and a slice of lime. I recall reading an article on Eudora Welty in which she described drinking one little glass of whiskey in the late afternoons before dinner. It was her small indulgence, a way to wind down at the end of the day with a cocktail. Similarly, at the end of the day, my father and stepmother, Jordan, whom I called Momma Jordan or Momma J, would share a glass of wine or a drink, and my father would read the day's mail and we'd speak about current affairs or anything else. We'd take our seats in the sunroom off the main room. It was all glass, and you had the impression that you were sitting outside.

I had several experiences with my mother's drinking. She was a secret drinker who drank in private. I didn't notice this until I was about eighteen years old, when I was visiting my mother in New Orleans and she came to the door slurring her words. She had always claimed that it was her meds. That was how I was used to viewing her. She had spent a significant amount of time in mental health facilities and therapy clinics, and she was on drugs. But it suddenly came to me during this meeting with her in New Orleans that she was also drinking extensively. I had no idea she was an alcoholic until that point.

Her mental disorder robbed her of her mother's instincts and abilities. We were tight till she died in 2004, but after that, we drifted apart. I didn't rely on her in any way. I realized at a young age that I would not receive from my mother what most children do: stability, warmth, dependability, and support.
Looking back, she is responsible for many of my positive characteristics. She went through everything. She enjoyed listening to music and playing the piano. She was a fan of Judy Garland, Erroll Garner, and Ray Charles. Joan Baez and Leonard Cohen

were also introduced to me by her. As I grew older and more conscious of her mental condition, I began to draw parallels between her position and that of Sylvia Plath, and in many respects, Anne Sexton. Plath and Sexton both committed suicide. My mother did not commit suicide, but she did disappear in other ways, at least in the eyes of her children.

My mother was obsessed with psychotherapy and devoured whatever book she could get her hands on about it. She went in and out of psychiatric hospitals and was always in therapy. Throughout my childhood, everything concerning my mother revolved around hospitals, therapists, and drugs.

My father was continually saying things like, "Your mother's not well, it's not her fault, your mother's not well, don't be mad at your mother." That was clear to me. He actually said something kind of kind about her.

Lucille Fern Day, my mother's name, was born on December 31, 1930. Reverend Ernest Wyman Day and Alva Bernice Coon Day were her parents. Her father was a Methodist clergyman, so strict that you'd believe he was Baptist. She had three older brothers and one younger brother. Her younger brother, Robert, was killed on his way home from World War II on his motorcycle. That was prior to my birth. My mother always told me that he was the sensitive one in the family. He was a poet and musician, like my mother. Robert, my younger brother, was named after him.

Mom studied music but never made a living from it. According to my knowledge, she began playing the piano at the age of four. She was smitten by it. But music became an albatross for her, and the piano became an albatross for her, because she wasn't allowed or able to pursue it as a career. But she struggled greatly because she did not have a musical career. It had an impact on her confidence, or lack thereof.

When I was a kid, we had a piano in the house. Mama carried a piano with her wherever she went after my parents divorced. However, the piano would come and go. It was both a thrill and a burden, a love-hate relationship. It was a toss-up; she couldn't live with or without a piano. She wasn't like Bette Davis in an old movie, rushing around with lipstick smeared on her lips. Her mental sickness was more subdued, subtle, and colossal all at the same time.

My mother told me that her family didn't have plumbing when she was a kid, so they used newspapers for wallpaper and insulation. They were all working-class people who didn't care about school or college. She had a sharp mind and enjoyed reading good literature. Her ability to break out and go to college and become a well-read person was a testimonial to her abilities because none of her relatives were like that at all.

My mother met my father while she was a music student at LSU. My father was despised by my mother's family. He was the guy who was a literary poet. Despite the fact that they were both from church backgrounds, his family was liberal and open-minded.

Later in life, my father informed me about my mother being sexually abused in horrible ways by her father and one or more of her older brothers while she was a child. My sister, Karyn, who attended therapy sessions with my mother when she was older, later verified this to me. Karyn withheld this information from me for many years, and I don't believe she made the wrong decision. Learning about this was unimaginably horrifying and heartbreaking, and I'm still processing it.

I remember my mother being happy and us being happy together. She had a wonderful sense of humour. We used to giggle at everything. But, like Sylvia Plath, she would wander in and out of her disease. My father told me that she was previously diagnosed with manic depression and paranoid schizophrenia.

She was admitted to mental facilities on occasion after having nervous breakdowns. My father used to claim that everything seemed OK with her when they were dating and before they married. They married, although they didn't have much money. My father was an itinerant professor who moved around and worked at several colleges. My mother was not working at the time because most women did all of their jobs at home.

On January 26, 1953, I was born in Lake Charles, Louisiana. You could say I was a natural fighter. I was born with spina bifida, which is obviously not the best condition for someone who will spend a couple of hours every night standing on a platform, but I've overcome it admirably. I was frequently ill as a child. My windpipe became obstructed when I was about a year old, necessitating an emergency tracheotomy. My difficulties persisted for another couple of years. I got croup and had to be hospitalized in one of those oxygen humidity tents, and then I was isolated at home in another oxygen tent in my bedroom.

My parents' relationship deteriorated after I was born, and my father always believed I received the short end of the stick. I was their first child, and the added obligations added new worries and tensions. My mother would go into these nasty moods when I was a child, and no one ever knew what caused or provoked it. My brother, Robert, was born two years later, followed by my sister, Karyn.

When I was a teenager and an adult, whenever I was having problems, my father would tell me, "Well, honey, once when you were three years old, before your brother and sister were born, I came home from work and your mother had locked you in a closet because you were being a typical three-year-old and crying and she couldn't handle it." That's how he explained my problems. He had a keen brain and was a big fan of Sigmund Freud. So dad was constantly analyzing things, and he would give me that tale to explain how things were for me as a child. He'd argue that Mom wasn't being cruel. She just couldn't handle it. She presumably thought locking me in the closet would keep me safe. When I think about it now, it seems dreadful. How could a mother do something like that? But my father was always there to remark, "She can't help herself. It isn't her fault. She's not feeling good."

When I was a baby and toddler, my mother used to tell me stories about how poor we were. She claimed she had to borrow bread from neighbors in order to feed us. They also didn't have a crib for me, so she took a drawer from my chest and made it into my bed. Poverty strained my parents' already strained relationship.

If a youngster spills something on the floor, a healthy family might respond, "Oh, that's okay, honey, we'll clean it up." "Goddamn it!" my mother would exclaim. My father wasn't perfect, either. He'd get irritable, and I never knew what kind of mood he'd be in. He'd tell me stuff like, "If you keep doing that, I'm going to knock your teeth down your throat."

But I bonded with my father in ways that I would not have if my mother had been more stable, if she had been more emotionally open to me. When my mother was very bad—yelling, screaming, cussing, throwing things at my dad or the wall—he'd take us out to play Putt-Putt or watch a drive-in movie, anything to get us out of the home. He assumed the position of what a mother would have done in those days. Despite this, I didn't grow up hating her or feeling anger toward her since my father always said, "It's not her fault." She's not feeling good."

I'm seventy years old and still dealing with a lot of stuff. I've avoided talking about my childhood for decades, instead writing songs about it, since I guess I came to accept it as normal. "OK, my mother is freaking out and yelling, and my father is having a bad day today."

One of my favorite images of my father and me is still in my possession. I'm maybe two years old. We're standing on our front steps, and it appears that we were getting ready to go to church, or that we had just returned from church, because he's wearing a suit and I'm wearing a small dress and a tiny jacket. It has a certain sweetness and purity to it. We're just standing on the front stairs together. As you can see, we had a great bond. My mother's mental condition had begun to rear its ugly head by the time I was born, so my father was taking care of me more and more.

Now that I've studied a lot of psychology literature and gone through considerable treatment and self-education on mental illness and dysfunctional families, I know that I had no method of recognizing or dealing with the trauma that occurred to me. Kids will eventually blame themselves. All of that energy has to go somewhere. You're the small kid sitting in the locked closet, wondering, "What did I do that was wrong?" My father then said, "It's not her fault, she's not well, you can't be angry at your mother." What was I going to do with all that grief, bewilderment, and rage?

When I was eight years old, not long after we relocated to Baton Rouge, I was referred to a child therapist. I dimly recall sitting in a room with this woman and playing some sort of board game. "Well, we were concerned that you might be, you know...because of your mother's illness," my father said. I don't believe I was acting out in any way. It was simply a precautionary measure. "We need to make sure everything is in order," he explained. Maybe my mother was having a particularly difficult time, and he was afraid I was being traumatized by it.

I was in a pub in New York a few years back when an older gentleman approached me and inquired what I was working on. I mentioned this book. He'd been involved in the music industry. "Don't write about your childhood," he said. Nobody wishes to read about it. Simply describe your music. Simply choose a topic from your professional experience to write about." But so many of my songs are inspired by my youth. Some listeners pick up on these recollections and emotions in my music. "Did you have a rough childhood?" a woman approached me after a show at the Dakota in Minneapolis. As I made my way backstage, I nodded my head. "I thought so," she admitted.

I recall spending the night with my cousins at my uncle and aunt's house in Baton Rouge. It was more like my parents throwing us out for a day or two to get rid of us. This was my mother's brother and his wife, as well as their twin daughters, who were constantly fighting. My aunt, their mother, was a devout Christian with jet-black dyed hair. She would tint the pancake batter with food coloring and make them all different colors.

When my mother's mother, my grandmother, thought we'd done anything wrong, she'd pluck switches from the hickory tree in their yard and beat us with them. I can't imagine how my mother felt growing up in that environment, suffering through the horrific trauma she did but also living among people who didn't follow the news or even know who the mayor or governor was. There are some of us who live in reality.

Forty years later, I penned "Bus to Baton Rouge," which appeared on my 2001 album Essence. Some people have said it's one of my most beautiful tunes, almost like a gospel hymn. It's without a doubt one of my most documentary tunes. It's about my mother's family and her parents' house in Baton Rouge, where we frequented.

My father used to say that we carry our origins forward, so telling my story and establishing my foundation must begin with my roots—my family and the individuals whose sensibilities and ideas I inherited. Despite the fact that my mother's family was so dissimilar, I can easily identify myself in my ancestors. My paternal and maternal grandfathers were both Methodist preachers, one in Louisiana and the other in Arkansas. Being a Methodist preacher requires you to go from church to church and community to community. So that's the life my mother and father knew as children. After they married, my mother and father moved our family from place to place in quest of fresh employment. Despite the fact that I was born in Lake Charles, Louisiana, my family did not stay there long. My brother was born when I was two in Vicksburg, Mississippi, and my sister was born when I was four in Jackson, Mississippi.

My father was a scientist who became a poet—not your conventional career path—and was always looking for teaching employment. He didn't get a full-time teaching position until I was eighteen. We had resided in twelve different towns since my birth. I can recall nine of them. Moving is said to be one of the most stressful events in one's life. I moved twelve times before the age of eighteen.

I've always felt at ease on the road, moving around to advance my career. It runs in my family. I feel at home on buses and in hotels, then standing in front of people, almost like a traveling preacher, and conveying what I believe most strongly, what I care most about, which is my music. And because so much of my music is about my life, it's like a story that is always being lived, narrated, written, and sung.

My father brought the souls of my paternal grandfather and grandmother, Ernest Burdette Williams and Ann Jeanette Miller Williams, into my life. His parents, in contrast to my mother's, were impressive folks. My grandfather had already worked as a teacher, a county tax assessor, a bank clerk, and a club baseball pitcher before becoming a Methodist minister in Hoxie, Arkansas. Stanley Miller Williams, my father, was born in Hoxie in 1930. He was the fourth of what would eventually be six children. My grandparents had already lost five children by the time he was born, two of whom died in the 1918 flu epidemic.

Ernest was a social democrat and a progressive minister. He insisted on allowing everyone, regardless of race, to sit in the congregation at every new church, which was contentious because it violated the time's segregation laws. In Fort Smith, Arkansas, my grandparents were once held at gunpoint by a man who claimed he needed to teach them "southern manners." My grandmother had apparently been observed conversing with black people while riding on one of the town's streetcars, and white people in that town weren't meant to do so.

My grandfather invited Harry Leland Mitchell to secret meetings in the basement of his church not long after my father was born. Mitchell was a socialist and a sharecropper who fought for improved sharecropper conditions from landowners. This was the beginning of the Southern Tenant Farmers' Union, which Mitchell created in 1934 to assist sharecroppers and tenant farmers in obtaining better bargains during the Great Depression. In the 1930s, it was one of the few unions in America that welcomed both white and black members.

Ernest also fought alongside other preachers against Arkansas's governor, Orval Faubus, in the 1957 public school crisis, when nine black students were denied admission to Little Rock Central High School. All of these stories—told and retold—were a significant part of the family lore on my father's side, and that's where my father got his progressive streak, and probably where I got mine. As a child, I would go to hear my grandfather preach and then discuss it with my father. I discovered a volume of my grandfather's printed sermons that my father had put together a few years ago in my father's possessions.

When I was touring with Bonnie Raitt in Vancouver in July 2022, my tour manager approached me one night and said there was an old man who would like to speak with me. Don Todd was a retired philosophy professor from Simon Fraser University. Growing up, he'd known my father and told me stories about him and my grandfather. Don told me that when my grandfather Ernest was younger, he was out walking on a trail when he noticed another small boy his age walking in the opposite direction. The young man was carrying a Bible and another in his bag. Ernest had an apple, which he exchanged for one of the children's Bibles. Most families in this section of Arkansas couldn't afford one, so this was a huge win. Ernest and this kid then got into a fight for whatever reason. Ernest then proceeded to beat up the boy and take back his apple, as well as one of the Bibles.

Ernest started reading the Bible. He could only read at a sixth-grade level, but it was enough for him to go through most of it and figure it out. He was set on fire by the Bible. My grandfather was a country boy who was a Christian liberal badass.

He was reading the Bible without the baggage of a church telling him what it was about. Ernest intended to become a minister while he was in his late teens. He became a radical Christian, backing unions and helping the needy as much as he could. In terms of money, not everyone was born equal. He wanted the poor to have greater resources, and he would go to any length to make it happen. He received his ordination somewhere in the 1920s. When the Great Depression struck in 1929, his feelings for the poor and his condemnation of the wealthy grew even greater. In the early days of the Depression, he met his wife, and my father was born in 1930.

Back then, large land firms owned farms that were administered by sharecroppers and tenant farmers, with the majority of the profits going to the owners. It was almost as bad as slavery. Ernest despised the situation and fought it, citing the Bible as support. We could definitely use more of that nowadays. Don told me that my father went to college in 1947 with the goal of following in his father's footsteps, but for some reason it didn't work out for him. It irritated him.

Don appeared in Vancouver that night like a gracious ghost, a soul from another universe. He helped me realize that my grandfather was more radical than I had previously realized. Woody Guthrie, if he had been a pastor, would have been like my grandfather. That made me happy.

My father, like his parents, was constantly on the go, forward and ahead, here and there for this new job or that new employment. He worked as a book salesperson for Harcourt, Brace, and also sold encyclopedias door-to-door before earning his degree in biochemistry. His early literary impulses can be seen there. He had always expressed a desire to be a writer. He had penned poems as a child. He went to Hendrix College in Conway, Arkansas, right after finishing high school, hoping to major in English, but as part of his entrance exam, he had to take an aptitude test with a psychologist. His tenacious love of writing and languages persisted until he discovered a means to make his goal a reality. Don Todd told me that my father had written him letters about his growing interest in poetry. He believed the poets were doing what his father, Ernest, had done via his ministry—teaching something that was essentially unknown to the rest of the world.

My father, like his father, was always involved in the battle against racial injustice. George Haley, the brother of Alex Haley, the author of Roots, was one of his closest and lasting friends. My father met George in 1951, while he was a graduate student at the University of Arkansas, and George was one of the university's first three black students admitted to the law school. My father befriended George after he was harassed and teased by some of the other pupils. When they were together, my father was labeled a "n—— lover," and bags of urine were thrown at them, among other humiliating experiences.

My father and George were very close as a result of all of this, and when I was born, he asked George to be my godfather. George's brother Alex later wrote a magnificent piece in Reader's Digest about their experience, and of course, I was born right at the end of it. One of my most treasured possessions is a black-and-white photograph of George Haley holding me as a newborn, which my father presented to me in this lovely antique silver frame.

When I declare, "I'm a southerner," many people think, "That must mean you're racist, this, that." There are so many stereotypes linked with being southern, which is a whole other issue. That's why my father taught me, "We are southerners, and we have to fight the people who think all southerners are racist, hicks, and stupid." That's how I was brought up. That's where I'm from.

One of my father's favorite anecdotes was about meeting Hank Williams in January 1953, a few months before I was born. He went to watch Hank perform in Lake Charles, where my folks were residing. He was shackled and determined to meet him later. My father admired Hank and his music, and I believe he felt a bond with him beyond the fact that they shared a last name. They also had a similar appearance—tall and lanky and gangly, with high cheekbones. It appears that they may have been linked.

After Hank's act, my father went over and introduced himself, and they ended up at a bar near the venue that Hank recommended. It was a gas station that offered alcohol; there were plenty of them back then. According to how my father narrated the tale, he and Hank were discussing how either of them had much money growing up. He told Hank about coming from Arkansas, growing up in a humble working-class home, his father being a Methodist preacher, and becoming a poet and beatnik college lecturer. Hank eventually asked my father what he wanted to drink, and my father requested bourbon and water. "Williams, you should be drinking beer because you have a beer-drinkin' soul,' " Hank replied.

Hank meant that, despite having a college education and becoming a professor, my father was still connected to that element of the working-class milieu. This was a story my father would tell over and over. Accepting and moving in both the world you were born into and the one you discovered on your own may have been the most significant lesson he ever taught me.
Hank died soon after, and I was born three and a half weeks later.

Chapter 2

My mother and father were a good match on the surface as well as in substance. She was a huge fan of the arts and was highly supportive of my father's passion for writing. We were living in Baton Rouge in 1961, and my father was selling refrigerators at Sears, Roebuck while looking for science teaching employment. But what he really wanted was to write. My mother and father attended a reading by poet John Ciardi, who, among other things, had done a famous translation of Dante's Divine Comedy. They were not invited to the reception following the reading, but people were too courteous to kick them off. My mother approached Mr. Ciardi and shook his hand, saying, "There is another great poet in this room tonight and you didn't even know it." "Who is it?" he asked. "How could I have been so blind?" "His name is Miller Williams," she explained. He's my fiance." My father was embarrassed by my mother's candor, but Mr. Ciardi requested that my father write him a few poems. Then, a month later, after my father had not yet mailed them, John Ciardi wrote to him, "Dear Mr. Williams, You were going to email me some poems—P.S. Tell your wife that I admire her approach." This would prove to be a watershed moment in my father's career as a writer. My father regarded John as a mentor and one of his longtime best friends. I believe I inherited some of my mother's bravery, which was shown in her readiness to confront Mr. Ciardi.

But, regrettably, my mother's illness was worsening, and she couldn't keep it together for long. There were a few mishaps. When we were in Baton Rouge, my father had a meeting with his LSU dean in our living room. He mistook my mother for sleeping and asked the dean over for a drink instead of holding the meeting in a more formal setting. Mama strolled sloppily into the room, incredibly inebriated, wearing only her underpants, in the middle of their discussion.

My mother had a nervous breakdown, screaming and yelling at my father, when I was about nine years old and we were living in

Baton Rouge. This was not long after she had been so supportive of John Ciardi during his reading. You can see how her mental illness made her unpredictable: anything, beautiful or dreadful, may happen at any time.

When my parents divorced, my mother asked if I wanted to live with her or with my father. I don't recall answering. I think I wanted to stay with my father. But I recall going into their closet and personally stroking their clothes—my mother's outfits and my father's shirts. That was all I could do at the time, and it provided me some solace.

My family was dysfunctional and messed up. But it isn't what matters to me. What counts is that I got my mother's musical aptitude and my father's writing ability. My stepmother showed me how to set a dinner party table with cloth napkins and silverware. Grandma Day also showed me how to make fertilizer for plants by combining coffee grinds and eggshells, as well as how to make banana pudding and fig pickles. And Pippaw taught me morality and diplomacy, while Mimmaw taught me church hymns. My family was lovely in certain ways.

I spent a lot of time at Uncle Bob and Aunt Alexa's house during those years, as my mother's mental illness worsened. My cousin Mac would spend the night at the home of a friend, and I would sleep in his bed. My father would drop me off there before dropping off my brother, Robert, to Grandma Day's place. She allegedly spoiled Robert.

My uncle Bob worked as a part-time actor in several plays and musicals at the Baton Rouge Little Theater. He helped me land a little part in a local production of Annie Get Your Gun, a popular musical for smaller theaters in the 1960s. During that show, I fell in love with the stage. This was perhaps a year or two before I began playing guitar. I felt a high like I'd never had before in front of an audience with other cast members, including my cousin Mac, Uncle Bob's son. I was sucked in. Bob, too, was often listening to musical soundtracks on his stereo at home. Oklahoma!, South Pacific, and more films come to mind.

Blind Pearly Brown was a blind preacher and street performer in Macon. Brown was on the sidewalk, singing and playing the guitar while collecting tips. I was standing there, clutching my father's hand. It was a memory I'd never forget. I was so taken with the music that my father purchased a CD of songs recorded by folklorist Harry Oster a few years later. When I initially received my guitar, the songs on the album were among the first I learnt. Songs like "God Don't Ever Change" and "You're Gonna Need That Pure Religion," which I had no idea was a traditional song at the time.

Years later, I looked at Blind Pearly Brown. A reporter cited him as stating in 1958, "I pray to the Lord that we will someday see a world without strife, when all of us can live as brothers." "I pray to the Lord that I may live to see the day when humanity is considerate of one another." Brown was reported in another piece in 1972 as saying, "It's not bad being a street singer." It will teach you something new. You should consider how certain people can be cruel to you."

This, to me, is the core of the blues. It's about making sense of your experiences and learning from them.

My father took me to Flannery O'Connor's residence in Milledgeville when we were in Macon. I was eight years old at the time. Harcourt Brace was the same publishing house that published some of O'Connor's books, so that's presumably how my father drew the link. He had sought her out in his ambition to become a writer. He regarded her as his most important teacher. She answered by inviting him to come and see her. As we approached, we noticed a circular dirt driveway in front of the two-story house.

When we arrived, the venetian blinds inside her front screen porch had been drawn. The housekeeper appeared on the porch and stated, "Miss Flannery isn't quite ready to receive guests." "Okay, Miss Flannery is ready to see you," the housekeeper remarked after a time. You are welcome to come in." My father entered and sat with her. I stayed outdoors while they were there, wandering around her yard and chasing her peacocks. Years later, I realized how significant this visit was. I consider myself fortunate to have maintained that recollection.

I was familiar with that kind of southern gothic experience from spending time with my mother's side of the family, and I believe that's why I adored Flannery O'Connor's writing. I first read her when I was sixteen, many years after that visit, when I was too young to appreciate anything she wrote. But when I was sixteen, I discovered something that felt genuine. I began reading her short stories and devoured them all. I immediately understood what she was saying.

My father would look up to O'Connor as a mentor. She would later assist him in obtaining a post teaching English at Louisiana State University in Baton Rouge.

My childhood was a jumbled mess. I was exposed to people like Blind Pearly Brown and Flannery O'Connor and learnt to value a person's aesthetic sensibility as something vital, something that distinguished and distinguished them. But I also had to deal with a lot of anguish, both physically and mentally.

My father came to one of my gigs at the Bluebird in Nashville when I first started playing this song in public. It was his first exposure to music. He approached me later, dressed in his typical college professor pants, shirt, tie, and sport coat, thin as always, with his beard and glasses. "I'm so sorry," he said. I'm very sorry." When I inquired what he meant, he replied, "That little girl crying in the backseat was you." I'll never forget that bittersweet moment. At the same time, I was astounded and moved. I had no idea I was writing about myself the whole time! It took a poet to point this out to me.

I hope I could be as academically astute in my songwriting as Bob Dylan is. But all I can do is write about my thoughts and the feelings of the world, and I believe this is what distinguishes my music. It incorporates elements of southern gothic, blues, folk, and rock.

My father and I had several chats about it. He never made me feel awful about not loving a certain writer or artist. For example, Faulkner was never a favorite of mine. I attempted to read him, but I couldn't stand him. Flannery O'Connor and Carson McCullers were my favorites. Because Faulkner was so revered at the time, I was hesitant to inform my father. "Oh, that's okay," he said when I eventually told him. You can read someone else's mind. There are many authors out there. You don't have to like them all." After a brief pause, he said, "Plus, Faulkner was an asshole."

Chapter 3

My parents' house was usually filled with music, and there were numerous literary parties. One of my father's favorite pastimes was throwing a party at our house after reading. My father would play southern soul albums by Wilson Pickett and Ray Charles whenever those celebrations got rolling. Ray's album Modern Sounds in Country and Western Music was a favorite of his. He was also a fan of Chet Baker, John Coltrane, Bessie Smith, and Lightnin' Hopkins. Of course, the early Folkways releases were crucial. I recall going to see some of my father's friends and hearing two CDs that became extremely important to me: Songs to Grow On volumes 1 and 2 by Woody Guthrie and Pete Seeger. The lyrics reflected their wit and humor. Even though they were children's songs, they had a profound and unique quality to them. Joan Baez, Vol. 2 was another important early record for me, which my mother introduced me to when I was about eight or nine years old.

My first memory of playing an instrument was on my mother's zither, which she owned since she was a child. It looked like an Autoharp, except you played it on your lap. You slid sheet music between the strings and it showed you how to play a song, similar to tracing a picture beneath a sheet of blank paper. You'd use your thumb on one hand and your fingers on the other. I was just getting started looking for something to do. I wanted to play the piano so I could sing songs.

My family went to Santiago, Chile, for a year when I was eleven years old, in 1964. A few years later, when I was seventeen, we would spend a year in Mexico City, and these two years immersed in Latino cultures left an indelible mark on me.

We traveled to Santiago because my father had earned an Amy Lowell Traveling Poetry Scholarship. He met and befriended Pablo Neruda and Nicanor Parra, two outstanding Chilean poets. My father was listening to local radio and bought Chilean albums. Nicanor became a close friend of my father, and his sister, Violeta Parra, was a great musician best known in America for her song

"Gracias a la vida," which Joan Baez recorded years later. Violeta sang and played acoustic guitar to Chilean folk music, but her influence stretched beyond Chile. She'd already recorded many records by the time we got to Santiago, which Nicanor delivered to my father. A documentary video dubbed her "the mother of Latin American folk music."

Her songs left a lasting influence on me. This lovely and powerful woman in her forties was playing guitar and singing folk tunes. Joan Baez was the only American lady I was aware of operating in that capacity at the time.

I had to wear a uniform to school there, which I despised as a schoolgirl. That immediately changed as I fell in love with the location, culture, and music. Those were turbulent times in Chile, but I didn't really understand what was going on until years after we left. Many surrounding nations were experiencing revolutions, but the turbulence in Chile was just getting started, with the violence rising over the next few years, eventually leading to Allende's overthrow in 1973. I've always remembered the tragedy of Victor Jara, a singer-songwriter and activist who was kidnapped by death squads. Before he was slain, his fingers were severed. It was one of the most frightening things I'd ever heard.

Violeta unfortunately committed suicide in 1967 after her lover was slain during the revolution. She shot herself with a gun when she was 49 years old. Nicanor informed my father of her death first. Looking back, the lyrics of "Gracias a la vida," recorded less than a year before her death, appear to be a suicide note.

I didn't know Violeta directly, but her brother Nicanor paid us a couple of visits in the States. So it felt like I knew her or was only a few steps away from her. She was the first person to whom I was related in any way to commit suicide, but she was not the last.

We returned to Baton Rouge at the end of my father's fellowship year in Santiago. I was immediately in over my head. In Chile, all the girls wore tight-fitting pants with no skirt over them. I owned several pairs of those pants, but when I wore them to school in

Baton Rouge, I was instructed to change my clothes because they were too tight. The principals and instructors believed the pants were inappropriate. They were totally good in Santiago.

My father met my future stepmother, Jordan, during my first year back in Baton Rouge. She was an LSU undergraduate in one of his seminars. He was 35 years old, and she was either eighteen or nineteen. I was twelve years old. My sister Karyn was eight years old, and my brother Robert was ten.

At the time, I was extremely protective of my younger siblings. My parents had not yet divorced, and my mother was still living in the house. Jordan entered the house as an extra guardian or babysitter, and everything changed. To say the least, it was an odd and unpleasant circumstance. I have photos of my mother and Jordan hanging out in the same room, seated at the dining room table. Jordan was supposed to come into the house and take care of the kids and save the family, which my mother, of course, despised. Something was going on between my father and Jordan, and you could tell she wasn't simply a professional maid or nanny. It wasn't typical. Here's this young girl, one of my father's college pupils, who is only six or seven years my senior, and there's something going on between them. But I didn't want to blame my father, who had been my rock throughout my life. I needed to hang on to something. I just tried to be as respectful as possible while ignoring the questions in my brain. It wasn't simple, though.

Jordan was so young that she didn't have the maturity to deal with the circumstances. My obsessive-compulsive disorder began the same year Jordan moved into our home. That's when I started picking at my skin. Adolescent hormones were presumably also starting to kick in. I wasn't a cutter like Dusty Springfield described herself in her memoirs, but I did cause some wounds and blisters.

My father took us on one of his outings outside the home one day to get away from my mother, who was experiencing a nervous breakdown. He took me to the drive-in, where the first film was I Was a Teenage Werewolf, starring Michael Landon, and the main attraction was Hush...Bette Davis in Hush, Sweet Charlotte. Both of those films terrified me, especially Hush...Hush, Sweet Charlotte, in which a cleaver severs someone's hand from their arm and Charlotte—Bette Davis—has blood all over her clothes. Then there's talk of beheadings, and Charlotte becomes drugged and has hallucinations.

What type of father would take his twelve-year-old daughter to watch this? Because of my mother, I know dad was frantic to get us out of the house. Hush grew on me as I grew older...Hush, Sweet Charlotte because it reflected the gothic South as I knew it from my mother's evangelical family, but it was set in a conventional southern home rather than that place in Baton Rouge. Same dysfunctional crazy dangerous crap concealed inside a gorgeous estate, filmed just a few blocks away from my mother's family's house where all this shit happened.

1965 was also the year I purchased my first guitar and began taking lessons. I can't emphasize how tumultuous that year was for me. I was on the verge of becoming a teenager, with everything that entails for any girl, and Jordan was now a member of the family; I was experiencing a whirlwind of emotions and desires. My teacher was a guitarist in a rock band in Baton Rouge. Years later, as an adult, I couldn't recall his name, but I remembered seeing a photo of him. I put those photos on social media while researching this book, and some friends and fans assisted me in tracking him down. Alan Jokinen is his name, and he currently resides in San Francisco. He had been a graduate student in poetry at LSU in Baton Rouge and had studied with my father. He studied poetry during the day and played in rock bands at night.

Alan used to come over to our house once a week. He had long blond hair and a rocker appearance. He was a thoughtful and polite man. We'd sit in the living room, and I'd tell him about a song I wanted to learn, and he'd show me how to play it. He taught me a fingerpicking, rolling approach that I still use today. Because I was obsessed with Peter, Paul, and Mary, I learned how to play "Puff the Magic Dragon." Alan demonstrated me chords and fingerpicking skills for any song I wanted, and then I practiced that song for the remainder of the week. The next week, I'd have another song ready for him to teach me, and he'd show me how to play it. My goal was not to become an accomplished guitarist, but rather to learn to play songs so that I could sing them.

When Alan and I met in 2020, he informed me that a professor hired him to drive his automobile from Fayetteville to San Francisco not long after my sessions with him ended and he finished graduate school. The professor had a new teaching position in the Bay Area. Alan drove their automobile across the country after his family flew to San Francisco. He returned the automobile and intended to stay in San Francisco for a few days. He never did leave, as it turned out. He found work there in a silk-screening company and subsequently launched his own store. He designed posters for Bill Graham, the Fillmore, and other clients. He's retired and still lives there.

I would go to music stores and look for songbooks after Alan taught me to play. I was always on the lookout for something. Because I couldn't read music, that was the only way I could learn. If I had a favorite record and discovered its songbook somewhere, I'd be overjoyed. I still recall the excitement of purchasing the songbook and the overwhelming desire to return home as soon as possible. I'd learn the chords and lyrics from the songbook, and the melody from the album. Joan Baez's Vol. 2, Judy Collins' Wildflowers, and The Beatles' 1965 were among my favorites. There was also the Folk Song USA songbook, which served as a sort of folk singer's bible at the time and which I still have. John and Alan Lomax gathered this massive collection of American folk music with English and Irish roots. The subtitle of the book is The 111 Best American Ballads. It includes songs such as "John Henry," "Skip to My Lou," "Little Brown Jug," "Down in the Valley," and "Oh! Susanna."

Another of my father's students visited the house during the fall semester of that year. He came in, clutching a record, and exclaimed, "Oh my God, you need to be listening to this." He put it on our record player. Highway 61 Revisited, Bob Dylan's latest album, was released at the end of August 1965. My head was utterly blown. I couldn't comprehend the words or the song titles, which included "Just Like Tom Thumb's Blues," "Queen Jane Approximately," and "Ballad of a Thin Man." What does that imply to a 12-year-old girl? It didn't make a difference. It hit me like a bolt of lightning, and I can still hear that record and feel the same way.

I had never heard of Bob Dylan before, but I had heard of Woody Guthrie and was familiar with the literary world of poetry thanks to my father. On this record, poetry collided with badass rock & roll. Dylan had taken elements from all of these universes and combined them for the first time. I was completely enthralled. I really liked the record cover, with his hair and the mysterious stranger standing there with a camera. That was the end of my story. I knew I wanted to be Joan Baez with her pants and little T-shirt, bare feet, and long hair after hearing that record. I knew I wanted to be in that world when I was twelve years old.

Dylan has had a profound impact on a long line of men and women. He was my musical partner and mentor. After hearing Highway 61 Revisited, I devoured his other CDs, Another Side of Bob Dylan and The Freewheelin' Bob Dylan. In some ways, he was my constant companion, my shadow, or I was his shadow. I wished I could be him in some way. I wished I could do what he was doing. I learned "Blowin' in the Wind" and "Don't Think Twice, It's All Right" from a young age. Also, "To Ramona," which is possibly my favorite Dylan song of all time. It's a love song for a woman.

As soon as I learned how to play the guitar, I spent almost all of my free time sitting around learning these tunes.

Chapter 4

Dad found a teaching post at Loyola in New Orleans a year or year and a half later, in 1966 or 1967, and we packed up and relocated yet again. I was thirteen or fourteen at the time. My parents had divorced by this point, and Jordan was about to become my stepmother. Mama also relocated to New Orleans, but she had her own apartment. My sister, brother, and I lived with my father and Jordan, but we paid regular visits to my mother. I couldn't have explained how twisted up and confusing that was for us kids at the time.

But we moved to New Orleans at the appropriate time for me. It was the ideal setting for a music-obsessed adolescent. Neil Young sings in one of his songs, "All my changes were there." He's talking about his childhood in Canada. That's how I feel about my fourteen to sixteen years in New Orleans. You have no idea how much music, and what kind of music, was flooding my mind.

I had guy friends mostly in New Orleans, and we all really liked music; that was our anchor. There weren't many girls who wanted to play music. I spent a lot of time hanging out at the home of two brothers, David and Cranston Clements, on Lowerline Street in Uptown near Tulane. I was dating a guy named Fielding Henderson, who used to play guitar in some high school bands with them and introduced me to them. I assumed they were significant since Fielding stated so.

I paid close attention to what he said. We adored each other and were just concerned with music and rescuing the world. We walked about New Orleans discussing current affairs, cultural tensions, and the latest album we'd heard. We still had a lot to learn. We were thirsty for information. I knew David and Cranston were soul mates when Fielding introduced us.

My family's house was on Robert Street in the Freret district, and David and Cranston's was about fifteen blocks down Willow Street. They quickly surpassed Fielding in importance. We could go over to David and Cranston's room and hang out. We'd fire up a joint and listen to the first album by Zeppelin, Buffalo Springfield, or the Doors, or Surrealistic Pillow by Jefferson Airplane, or Dylan, the Band, or Neil Young. We'd take in everything. The Beatles, the Stones, and Jimi Hendrix. David and Cranston's mother would return home from work with a six-pack of Budweiser or Dixie beer and a pack of smokes, remaining in the background. There were no such rules. We'd leave the house baking and spend hours walking down New Orleans' sidewalks—Lowerline, Maple Street, Decatur Street, the Quarter, and everywhere else.

David and Cranston both participated in high school bands and knew a lot of other musicians. Sometimes thirty kids would gather at their house to listen to music, smoke marijuana, and drink beer, though it was largely dope. It was easier to find pot than it was to get booze if you were underage.

We would sometimes skip school to listen to a new record. We could also take the St. Charles Streetcar into downtown. There was a record store called Weinstein's and another store called Smith's Record Center. We used to buy records whenever we had money. We'd spend our time in the French Quarter. We were teens strolling about observing and taking in everything. Buster Holmes' Bar and Restaurant was a restaurant. Clarence "Buster" Holmes reigned supreme over red beans and rice. Going there was a rite of passage for any New Orleans kid growing up. David, Cranston, and I would find seventy-five cents, walk up to the Buster's take-out screen window, and order three plates of red beans and rice for twenty-five cents each. We'd eat outside on the sidewalk.

One of my favorite memories from that time is my father taking us to Preservation Hall to watch a woman named Sweet Emma play the piano and sing. It reminded me of what it must have been like to listen to Memphis Minnie in the 1930s and 1940s. Sweet Emma sang raw jazz and blues songs. There was no air conditioning, so I'd sit there sweating while listening to her. Sweating through your clothes is common in New Orleans.

When we were walking around the Quarter one day, Jimi Hendrix came by on a flatbed truck, throwing out Mardi Gras beads and promoting his impending gig. Needless to say, witnessing Hendrix when I was fourteen was a tremendous thing for me. I went with a friend, and my father drove us there. Tulane University's football stadium served as the venue for the show. The field had a makeshift stage and a large crowd, but the bleachers were far distant from the stage. However, it was unforgettable.

One night, there was a particularly large crowd at David and Cranston's house, and several black youngsters were present. The gathering spilled into the front yard, and someone phoned the cops since there were black children present. The police arrived and halted the festivities. When David and Cranston's father found out, he was incensed that his sons were hanging out with black kids. They were expelled from high school, and one of their friends stole his father's car, and they all drove to California. They had each saved his allowance for the vacation, but they still didn't have enough money to accomplish anything. They got as far as El Paso, Texas, before being apprehended by police after one of them stole a bottle of Coca-Cola from a petrol station.

My father, on the other hand, had always been politically active and progressive. As a teenager in New Orleans, I used to stand in front of the grocery store and hand out "Boycott Grapes" pamphlets for Cesar Chavez, and I'd bring my guitar and play songs at protests whenever I could. I learnt all the protest songs, including Dylan's "Universal Soldier" and Donovan's "Universal Soldier." I was reading novels like Eldridge Cleaver's Soul on Ice and Malcolm X's Autobiography. Everything in the world was on fire. There were the assassinations of JFK, RFK, MLK, and Malcolm X. Cops shot children on college campuses who were protesting the Vietnam War. I'd cry as I saw news videos of these events.

I was expelled from high school twice for taking part in protests. All the excellent schools in New Orleans were Catholic at the time, but I went to Fortier, pronounced "for-shay," a French name that everyone mispronounced "for-tee-er." It was overcrowded and understaffed, and the principal was a clear racist, despite the fact that it had recently been integrated.

One morning, I was booted out for the first time before the bell sounded. My friend asked if I would distribute leaflets from Students for a Democratic Society around campus. SDS leaflets were student-created lists of grievances and demands. When a black student and a white student got into a fight at school, the black student was sent home while the white student was not. We were demanding that such uneven treatment cease. I was discovered passing out pamphlets and was sent to the assistant principal's office along with two other students. The assistant principal chastised us and threatened to expel us from school if we did it again.

The Pledge of Allegiance would be played over the loudspeaker every morning in the homeroom. You were meant to rise up and say the vow while placing your hand over your heart. I opted to stand, but not to say the pledge or place my hand over my heart. My two friends agreed not to do it either. We were apprehended and sent back to the assistant principal's office.

We were put on indefinite leave. I informed my father what had happened when I arrived home. "Don't worry," he said. We'll get you back into school with the help of an ACLU lawyer." He did, and I was allowed to return to school. "Try to stay out of trouble for the rest of the year," my father said.

I tried my hardest, I honestly did. But a few weeks later, when I arrived at school one morning, there was a massive anti-racism rally going on, with a large march around the school. The NAACP was present, as was SDS. My progressive buddies noticed me through the window and cried, "Come on down!" I couldn't help myself. My heart was racing and I was thinking, "I have to go down there." So I dashed out of class and joined the march. The officers arrived and began tossing people into paddy trucks. I was able to escape and return home.

Everyone implicated was placed on indefinite leave. To be permitted back into school, you had to go to the principal's office and swear that you would never participate in another protest again. That was not going to happen. My father concurred. "The hell with that," he muttered. You're not going to learn anything there anyway." So I spent the remainder of the year essentially homeschooled. Dad was a teacher at Loyola and arranged for me to sit in on several of his classes. This was my final year of school.

I'm still in touch with David and Cranston after more than fifty years. My husband, Tom, and I will see them whenever we are in New Orleans. David eventually opened Snake and Jake's Christmas Club Lounge, which is now one of New Orleans' most famous dive bars. By building this bar, David has essentially recreated the old free-form house party of his youth. Cranston rose to prominence as a guitarist in New Orleans, working with everyone from Dr. John to the Nevilles to Irma Thomas.

Mama always found these fantastic large antique New Orleans apartments. One location was on Carrollton Avenue, close to St. Charles. She had a fantastic record collection, which I assisted her in expanding. Concert by the Sea by Erroll Garner was one of her favorite records. To me, the sheet music appeared to be a mystical mystery.

My brother, Robert, would frequently visit our mother's house and play the piano. He was quite talented and could play for hours on end. Mama was a big fan of Judy Garland and Sammy Davis Jr. I believe she resonated with Garland's well-known personal issues. But I was so young and preoccupied with my own life at the time that I couldn't realize how awful her mental health was.

But I loved her wholeheartedly. We used to go thrifting together sometimes. Mama enjoyed a good deal and was very proud of the furniture she'd purchased at the local St. Vincent de Paul thrift store. She had a terrific sense of humor and could make a lifelong friend in less than five minutes.

As my financial situation improved, I felt good about being able to assist her in her later years. One year, I assisted her in purchasing an automobile. Her health eventually deteriorated, and I was forced to assist her in moving into an assisted living facility I located in Fayetteville, Arkansas, which she grew to enjoy. Robert and Karyn were present, as were Dad and Mama Jordan, to keep an eye on her. My father and mother Jordan never abandoned my mother.

Chapter 5

My family packed their belongings and relocated to Mexico City for a year in 1970. My father held a fellowship at one of the universities there. We rented a two-story yellow house in the city's Distrito Federal neighborhood. The house included a housekeeper who resided in the backyard with her daughter. I would have been a junior, but I couldn't get into that high school. If I recall well, I was denied admission to school since I couldn't gather my proper papers owing to being tossed out of high school in New Orleans.

As a result, I spent most of that year solely playing guitar. I wasn't very interested in anything else. I wouldn't do something if I wasn't interested in it. I loathed PE class in high school, so I would just sit on the sidelines and accept zeros. But if I was passionate about something, such as guitar, I was willing to devote my entire day to it. I read good literature while I wasn't playing guitar. While we were living in Mexico City, I recall reading Camus' The Stranger. But I basically just listened to albums and played guitar.

Trouble had erupted during political demonstrations in Mexico City about a year before we moved there. The government had given the demonstrators permission to protest, but the military and police surrounded them and opened fire. People were either murdered or dragged away. During the year we stayed there, we met several people who had friends or relatives who had gone missing and had no idea what had happened to them. That made me nervous.

There was a small park not far from our house where I met some of the local young hippies. I'd hang out with them and smoke marijuana. They were continuously urging me to visit Oaxaca for the mushrooms.

Because of Vietnam, the politically leftist, younger, progressive liberals in Mexico City were anti-American, so we had to try to break down that first instinctual barrier in order to make friends with them, which was difficult. People who weren't anti-American were stiff and conservative, and we weren't their type, so we couldn't have the literary home parties my father loved to give. It was not like Santiago, where we had met numerous poets and writers. We invited all of our American friends to come visit us in Mexico for the entire year, and most of them did.

My mother was unable to visit, but I kept in touch with her via mail and phone. In New Orleans, she worked as an administrative assistant for an insurance business, largely answering phones. She appreciated hearing the stories and attempting to assist others; perhaps it helped to alleviate her own sadness.

Clark Jones, a close family friend from New Orleans, was one of our visitors. He was a nice and soft-spoken pianist. He reminded me of a youthful Pete Seeger. He could play the guitar, banjo, dulcimer, Autoharp, and ukulele, and he knew every folk song in the book—all the tunes I wanted to learn. He was a folk music historian who seemed to be able to narrate the story of America by playing old folk songs. He was around ten or fifteen years my senior, but we would sit about the house in Mexico City all day, playing one folk tune after another.

My father had invited two people from the American embassy over one night when Clark was there. Clark and I were performing folk songs when one of the two remarked, "We should send Cindy"—yes, I was called Cindy back then—"and Clark out on the road to play some shows around Mexico."

It turned out to be a life-changing experience for me. The embassy and the US Information Agency organized thirty shows for us across the country. We packed Clark's car and went around Mexico, staying in hotels that the embassy had reserved for us. We primarily performed traditional American folk songs with Dylan and Peter, Paul, and Mary songs at high schools or colleges. The government officials thought it was a good way to spread American goodwill throughout Mexico at a time when America was not popular, and that it would show the Mexican people that America wasn't just about bombs and the military, but that we had a folk cultural tradition similar to theirs. The embassy described our performance as "Folk Music from Spiritual to Protest with Clark Jones and Cindy Williams."

This was the first time I'd ever performed live, in front of an audience of strangers, and it was both nerve-racking and exciting. From the age of twelve to seventeen, I spent much of my time playing guitar by myself or in a living room with friends and family. Now I was standing in front of a large crowd, sometimes with Clark in a duo, sometimes by myself.

I recall playing a couple performances in San Miguel de Allende, which is an artists' colony in a gorgeous setting. Painters, artisans, musicians, and writers were among those in attendance. I was astounded at how well we were handled. Following the performance, I was given a bunch of flowers.

Clark went to North Carolina after performing with me in Mexico for several months, where he continued his instructional folk music presentations. He would email us press clippings from his shows. He'd perform at state parks, YMCAs, and municipal events. Through songs, he portrayed the narrative of the North Carolina coast. Another time, he put together a program of plant-related folk songs and performed them at the North Carolina Botanical Garden. I still have all of these Clark newspaper clippings in my scrapbooks.

When I look back on my life, I see a series of guardian-angel-type characters who gently but firmly helped me get my craft and career in order. Clark was among the first of these individuals. He was a lovely person with a large, loving heart. I was supposed to be in high school when I was traveling around Mexico with Clark, playing folk music. It provided me with an education that no school could have provided.

Chapter 6

In the 1960s, we would spend most of our summers in Middlebury, Vermont, attending the Bread Loaf Writers' Conference, which was like the Woodstock of writers' conferences. For a time, it was managed by John Ciardi, who took my father into the fold and appointed him to the faculty. During the day, younger writers' work was assessed in workshops, followed by free time to work in the afternoon. Everyone gathered in the evenings at the Barn, a large ancient building with a massive fireplace. There was basically one long party with everyone drinking and relishing together in between readings by recognized writers. To be invited to Bread Loaf, young writers had to go through a rigorous application process.

During those years, I became interested in a few different poets. One year, I fell obsessed with a poet named John who had blondish hair. We spent some time together throughout the nighttime partying. Nothing transpired between us save long discussions about music and literature, yet those discussions were crucial to me. We kept in touch through letters, and we'd meet each other again at Bread Loaf the next summer. He was modest and sensitive, yet he was an artist.

A few years later, I was living in San Francisco—it had to have been 1974, so I would have been twenty-one at the time—when I received a phone call from a mutual buddy I'd also met at Bread Loaf who said, "John took his own life." This was the first suicide of someone I knew very well on a personal basis. I started taking notes about it and remembered Violeta Parra.

A man in his twenties pulled his automobile up next to me one day in broad daylight. He got out and asked for instructions, or something along those lines. I was taken off guard. Then, all of a sudden, he dragged me into a ravine beside the road. He knocked me to the ground. I knew he was going to rape me. I could only think, "I hope he doesn't kill me" and "I hope he doesn't have a knife and stab me." Then something occurred to me—my fight, flight, or freeze system instinctively kicked in—and I became utterly still. "Would you please get off of me?" I asked calmly. This was not anything I did on purpose. It happened quite recently. When I said that, he stood up and apologized profusely. "I'm so sorry, I'm so sorry." Then he inquired if I needed a ride to my destination. I replied, "No."

He drove away, and I returned to the Barn, where my father was. I recall approaching him as he sat with other writers, conversing and drinking. "Don't let Karyn walk outside by herself," I said into his ear. My sister was about twelve years old at the time. "What are you talking about?" he asked. I informed him of what had occurred.

My father phoned the cops, and I tried to describe the man and his car, which appeared to be antique. Nothing ever occurred. Nobody was ever apprehended by the police. I experienced very uncomfortable feelings for a long time after that attack—shivering, shaking, upset stomach—every time I saw an antique vintage car that looked like the one this man drove.

When I was in my twenties, I was travelling down the interstate when my automobile broke down. When a man approached me, I assumed he was coming to help, but as he came closer, I noticed he had a massive erection poking out of his pants. I got into the car and shut the doors. He just stood there with this erection outside my window, asking if I needed assistance. He eventually left.

These occurrences left me traumatized. I was left with a scar or a wound. I was left feeling a little more fearful and skeptical. But it's nothing compared to what my mother went through. I'm shocked she held it together as well as she did now that I know more about what happened to her as a child.

When we returned from Mexico in 1971, I was eighteen years old, and my father was given tenure at the University of Arkansas in Fayetteville. He had finally arrived. He was content. My father and Jordan bought a house in Fayetteville and remained there for the rest of their lives after moving to twelve different towns in the first eighteen years of my life. Jordan is still residing there. She's lived in that residence for the past fifty years.

My father and a writer named Bill Harrison established an MFA program at the institution, which quickly became one of the best in the South, if not the country. Jim Whitehead, another writer, was an integral component of the show. It felt like every writer in the country came through for readings and workshops. The program had enough money to bring everyone to town. I recall seeing James Dickey, John Stone, and John Little.

My father would hold the classes in our home. At 5:00 p.m., the classes transitioned into parties. That's when they'd pull out the beer, drugs, and whatever else they could find and pump up the music on the stereo. The beautiful thing about Fayetteville is that you can contact your friends at 3:00 p.m. and say, "We're having a party at 5:00 p.m.," and they'll all show up. Five o'clock was the magical hour when it was permissible to begin drinking. I've never had anything like that happen to me since, although I've travelled to a lot of places as a musician and artist. Nothing compares to the chaotic Fayetteville literary drinking and partying culture. People believe that musicians are always wild, crazy, drunk, and fucking each other. From what I've seen, musicians are nothing like writers, not even close.

When I was thirty-one years old and had recently moved to Los Angeles, I decided to drive up to San Francisco to look for Charles Bukowski, among other things. I admired his writing and had recently moved to California, so it felt like a logical fit. When I told my father about it, he responded, "Well, honey, you know that he'll probably try to screw you." That phrase is no longer used. What father would say that to their 31-year-old daughter?

I started using birth control at the age of eighteen and never considered becoming a mother. Not even once. Growing up, I never witnessed any families truly appreciate their children. As a teenager, I recall thinking, "Wow, nobody seems to like having kids." Nobody appears to enjoy having children. It's a burden, not a pleasure." Everyone seemed to prefer partying and freely fucking each other. Family commitments and responsibilities didn't appear to matter to anyone, so why should they have mattered to me?

My father and stepmother's house was often full of interesting visitors. I liked that environment, and after leaving home and being on my own, I began to miss it greatly. I tried to recreate it, but I was never able to do so, even with all of the musicians I knew. I missed the literary world, the thought-provoking conversations, the cocktails, the wit, the warmth, the savvy qualities, and the beauty.

Dad also began a poetry workshop at the Cummins Unit in Gould, Arkansas. Another writer, Bob Ward, came to visit us one day, and Dad invited Bob and me to accompany him on one of his visits to the prison. I took my guitar and performed for the women's unit inmates. It was a terrible prison where they would later execute people. Needless to say, it was a once-in-a-lifetime opportunity.

A woman named Louise was one of my favorite visitors to our home at the time. Her husband had previously taught art at the university level. She was in her early nineties yet still looked very young. Her beauty captivated me. She always came over for the holidays, drinking gin and tonics and dancing to Wilson Pickett's music on my father's stereo. She must have had a strong constitution. She showed me that even in my nineties, I could be beautiful and even seductive.

Louise and her husband resided in a log cabin in the woods north of Fayetteville. I once went to see her while she was sorting through her belongings and cleaning out her closet. She handed me many items of jewelry as well as hair barrettes. The turquoise and other natural stones were stunning. Someone subsequently told me that she knew she was dying and had invited me to her house to say farewell. A few months later, she died. I miss her terribly.

Despite the fact that I never completed high school, my father was able to get me into the University of Arkansas, which I attended once we returned from Mexico. I discovered Andy's on Bourbon Street, which was searching for singer-songwriters to play regular sets for tips. Artists would sign up to perform at specific times, such as 8:00 p.m. to midnight or 9:00 p.m. to 1:00 a.m. I auditioned and was hired as a regular at Andy's. I was overjoyed. My first full-time job. I played sets for a few weeks and made decent money. It was enough to cover a month's rent, which was roughly $85 per month back then if you shared a place with someone. I was meant to return to campus, but instead I contacted my father and told him about the job. "Honey," he continued, "if you want to stay and do that instead of going back to school, that's fine with me." I was overjoyed. That has always struck me as a watershed moment in my life. What if my father had told me, "No, you have to return to college"?

I met several elderly males who lived in a big, rambling mansion while playing at Andy's and sharing an apartment with a stripper. They asked me to several dinner parties where there was a lot of marijuana smoking. It was Hippie Heaven. I was at a dinner party one night when I noticed a woman seated across from me wearing no shirt. There is no summit. We were in the 1970s, during the height of the women's liberation movement.

I also recall lying on a bed with a guy, smoking joints and listening to Nina Simone in that place. The music and cannabis scents permeated the place. The doors and windows were all open. "I love Nina Simone's music," I remarked, dreamily listening. I want to one day be able to do what she does." "You'll never be able to do that," he said. You'll never make it to where she is." He was making fun of me. I walked away and never returned to that house.

Soon later, a wonderful man named Zac joined my life. He was lanky and slender, with wavy blond hair and a large wide grin. He was childish, but in a good manner. We hung out and laughed all throughout New Orleans, which made him even more valuable to me. He didn't have a macho demeanor or anything like that. He was all about love, peace, and beauty, a true hippy rather than a chauvinist masquerading as a hippie.

I'd wanted to try LSD for a long time, but I'd been told to wait until I was eighteen. Zac and I decided to go on a trip together after my birthday. We spent much of our time in his room, with the windows open and music playing, rolling around naked on his bed and a blanket on the floor. We were hallucinating, giggling, and teasing each other. We didn't have a care in the world. It was fantastic. I possessed a copy of Ram Dass's Be Here Now, a renowned yogi and spiritual teacher at the time. I carried that book about with me like it was a Bible. I was on a spiritual journey. I was researching several routes and religions, with the exception of Christianity, with which I could not connect.

Chapter 7

I went to Nashville in 1972 to audition for Opryland. My dad's friend, Tom T. Hall's bass player, arranged for me to come there and audition, as well as put me up for a bit.

I didn't get through the audition, but I chose to stay a bit longer. I was going to bars at the time, and one night I went to the Exit/In, which is still open. There was a whole scene going on at the Exit/In; Guy Clark and Townes Van Zandt were both living in Nashville at the time and were part of it. I also met a weird guy named Wrecks Bell, who played bass, and his sidekick, Mickey White, who played guitar. We became fast friends, and they offered me to live in this enormous house with a bunch of musicians.

I met this guitarist one night at the Exit/In, and we asked him over to our house, where we sat around and played music while drinking Southern Comfort and smoking marijuana. The cops arrived at the door and we responded, and they came in and began searching the entire house for weed, which they could easily have smelled. They discovered a stockpile and a pot pipe in my room, so everyone was brought in except Wrecks, who managed to escape. We arrived at the station, and they eventually let everyone go except for myself and this guy named Skinny Dennis, so we spent the night in the county jail.

I recall the artist Rodney Crowell becoming involved in all of this as well; I believe he was going to move into the house, so he and a couple of the people who were living there were attempting to raise bail for us. We did leave the following day—one night in such an environment was enough for me. But my father was certainly aware of what was going on at this point because I needed him to post bail. We hired Rose Palermo, a lawyer with a reputation for being "understanding" to musicians.

Skinny Dennis, God bless him, agreed to take the blame; he was older and I wasn't even twenty, so I guess he figured it wouldn't be too awful for him. Forty-plus years later, in 2012, I was on tour in

Canada when this pot bust appeared on my record. I'd been to Canada a thousand times by this point, and it had never been an issue. But it became a serious issue that day; they were now giving me the third degree about the reason for the arrest. When they asked how much pot was found in my room, I replied, "None—it was just a pipe." That response had to be repeated multiple times.

They told me I needed to contact someone in Nashville to prove it wasn't a possession charge. My tour manager made contact with someone in Rose Palermo's office, who informed me that records in Nashville were destroyed after a set number of years, and that the arrest record was long gone. That appeared to be sufficient to satisfy the border patrol. I'm still not sure how that ended up on my record after all these years, especially because I wasn't charged with anything.

The silver lining to the story is that Wrecks and Mickey would play on my Happy Woman Blues CD a few years after we were jailed.

And here I was, having never completed high school and attempting to be a professional musician in my twenties, feeling like a fuckup the majority of the time. Then there was the hippy culture of the 1960s and 1970s to contend with, and I battled to find my place in society.

I believe that meeting some older blues musicians when I arrived in Austin in 1974 helped to liberate me from a lot of the exclusive and confining southern Christian guilt and hippie nonsense. I was dating Rich Layton when he landed a position as the sound engineer for the Blues Caravan, a traveling blues revue. Pinetop Perkins, Furry Lewis, and Big Memphis Ma Rainey were among the musicians. They invited me to join them. I didn't participate; I just tagged along.

Furry Lewis had a suit coat with spacious pockets in which he kept a pint of whiskey. He was in his early eighties. He was born in the 1890s. I was struck by how carefree he appeared to be.

At the time, I was beating myself up with all these guilty ideas, some of which were true and others of which were made up in my head. Around the same period, I spent one night at Mance Lipscomb's house in Navasota, Texas, which is in the middle of nowhere between Austin and Houston. Mance is regarded as a Texas country blues legend. He was born in Navasota in 1895 and spent his entire life there. He was born into a sharecropping family and later became one himself.

I'd been hanging out with this guy named Kurt Van Sickle, who had taken over as Mance's manager. Kurt was also a singer and songwriter. He asked whether I wanted to accompany him to meet Mance. Of course, I replied, it would be an honor. For many years, I had been listening to and learning from Mance's recordings. So Kurt and I drove out to his house and met Mance at a bus stop. Mance was hungry, and he remembered a greasy spoon that had amazing BBQ. So we came to a halt at this dive.

I was working at a health food store in Austin at the time and trying to eat well. I've worked at various health food stores and juice bars throughout the years, and I still strive to consume good cuisine.

We walked out of the restaurant and drove to Mance's residence. It was on the farm where he had spent the majority of his life. He also told us that he used to play Saturday night dances with his father, who played the violin. Then he began performing those dances solo or with his own band in what he referred to as "beer joints" and "juke joints."

Mance's wife was introduced to us. They had been together for about sixty years. Mance was this small little boy, and she was huge and powerful, with a deep, loud voice. We ended up sitting around and singing songs while playing music.

Many of these bluesmen are adamant about not being given credit for tunes they wrote. They don't put up with fools very well. Mance performed "Key to the Highway " for us and asserted that he wrote it in the 1920s or 1930s. That music is now deemed public domain and is not attributed to anyone. The first version I heard was Big

Bill Broonzy, and later Eric Clapton made it famous as a rock song. "Key to the Highway" was performed at Duane Allman's funeral in Macon, Georgia. Mance said he wrote it. That night at his place, he performed a couple other well-known songs that he said he wrote but was never given credit for. I trusted him.

Kurt and I awoke the next morning to find Mance's wife preparing bacon, fried eggs, and fried potatoes on the stove. It was the kind of breakfast hippies claimed you shouldn't have. The hippy breakfast consisted of granola and yogurt. I recall seeing Mance's wife prepare this breakfast for us and thinking about how the hippy lifestyle could be scary and restrictive in its own right. The blues musicians either taught me to be irrepressible or inspired me to embrace my irrepressible streak.

Chapter 8

Throughout my adolescence in the late 1960s, my father was vehement about cigarettes, sex, and birth control. But I never took to cigarettes, and I'm so glad I didn't because not smoking has allowed my singing voice to mature and expand throughout my life and career. Today, I believe my singing is as powerful as it has ever been. I don't sound like I used to; it's different, but just as nice, at least to me.

I've been referred to as an "erotic" songwriter. I don't disagree, but even though I used to have a lot of sex, I was never promiscuous. I was always partnered. Some didn't stay long, but I wasn't sleeping around at random. A nice discussion is frequently more memorable than fucking. That's what my song "Something About What Happens When We Talk" on the Sweet Old World album was about.

In the spring of 1978, I met Frank. At the time, I was twenty-five years old. I had been living in Houston and Austin, playing my trade and craft in their music scenes and working odd jobs in restaurants and health food stores to make ends meet. Frank had attended the University of Arkansas in Fayetteville and studied poetry in my father's department, but I don't believe he graduated. He was a legendary character in Fayetteville literary circles, but he never made a reputation for himself outside of the city. My father pushed Frank to work on poetry translations from foreign languages, but I'm not sure how close their professional connection was. Frank had already published many volumes of poetry by the time I met him, but he was making ends meet as a land surveyor. A land surveyor who wrote poetry...that's the kind of mix in a man I like.

Frank was 29 years old and married to a beautiful, intelligent painter named Ginny Crouch. Frank was also living with another gorgeous, intelligent woman, poet Carolyn "C. D." Wright, on the side. In Fayetteville, he and Carolyn co-founded a publishing company. Married to one while living with the other—an ad hoc, part-time devotion to both—was a strange arrangement.

Frank had just finished an enormous poem called The Battlefield Where the Moon Says I Love You when I met him. His writing was wild and raging. Everyone in town was hailing him as the next great American poet. He knew a lot about blues and country music, and I believe his poetry reflected that, as well as the Flannery O'Connor southern gothic style.

I thought him to be irresistible, as did many other ladies and men. Everyone wanted to be near him. He resembled Jack Kerouac and a southern rural lad. He was stocky and muscular, built like a wrestler or a rodeo performer. He was both charismatic and intriguing, swashbuckling and compassionate. When you see images of him, you can see why ladies fell in love with him.

I was smitten by him, in love with him. I'm not sure what you'd call our relationship. I wouldn't call it a love triangle or a love square with me, Ginny, and Carolyn because Frank and I never had sex. We simply hung out and talked. My relationship with Frank lasted around two months until he committed suicide by shooting a firearm into his chest. There are several versions of what happened leading up to his suicide.

Essentially, all of the stories agree that Ginny and Carolyn had had enough of Frank's philandering and faced him simultaneously, almost like an intervention, and he couldn't handle it. He had been out of town for a few weeks before this happened. When he arrived from this specific trip, Ginny and Carolyn awaited him. They informed him that they had discovered his game and that he had to choose one of them and stay with it, or they would both leave him. He went down the street to a friend's house to get a weapon, then returned home and shot himself. The whole incident had the feel of a Shakespearean tragedy.

Frank had sent me flowers to my father's house, which came on the day he committed suicide. I'm not sure if he sent them on the same day or the day prior. I received the flowers, but I never saw him again. He sent the flowers to let me know he was thinking about me while he was away.

Ginny and Carolyn's first phone call was to my father. They invited him to come over and assist clean up the bloody mess. From my perspective, my song "Pineola" very well describes the rest of the story. I spent years working on this song, which was released in 1992, fourteen years after Frank's death. Sometimes it takes that long to perfect a song.

The part of Frank's burial that still haunts me today, and which is mentioned in "Pineola," is that there was a large attendance of his friends and followers, but his family didn't know any of them, and vice versa. At Frank's tomb, two separate universes collide for the first and only time. I can't get that image out of my head.

The mythology of Frank Stanford grew after my song was out and I gained greater prominence in my career. New editions of his books were released. People began looking into him and his work. Some individuals have told me that my music sparked Frank's attention, but I'm not convinced. It could have just been a coincidence. A writer called me once, maybe thirty or thirty-five years after Frank died, and said he'd been digging through Frank's files at Yale University and that my name appeared in them. He said Frank wrote, "I feel free." I've been spending time with Lucinda, and she makes me feel more liberated." That made me happy, but it was also unsettling. This writer implied that Frank and I had this stormy affair, which is not true.

Frank's suicide occurred four years after the suicide of my Bread Loaf companion. My thoughts and feelings about those two deaths evolved into the song "Sweet Old World," which was also the title of my 1992 album, which contained "Pineola." It took me a dozen or more years to perfect those two songs and record them.

Frank's obituary appeared in the Grapevine, a free weekly newspaper in Fayetteville. I clipped it and kept it in my scrapbook, which I still have now.

I had signed my first record contract three weeks before Frank died. On May 12, 1978, I signed a contract for $300 to make a record for Folkways Records.

Chapter 9

When I was living in New Orleans in 1972, I met another singer-songwriter named Jeff Ampolsk, and the seeds for my Folkways album deal were planted. We stayed in touch, and he recorded an album for Folkways a few years later. I was aware of Mo Asch's iconic label, which is now part of the Smithsonian Institution, but I never imagined I'd be able to record for them. In early 1978, Jeff and I were conversing, and he remarked to me, "If you send a cassette demo to Mo, I bet he will make a record for you."

I was skeptical, but Jeff persuaded me to do it and gave me the address. I prepared a cassette of the songs I'd been playing in gigs and mailed it to Mo. These songs were interpretations of classics by artists such as Robert Johnson, Memphis Minnie, Hank Williams, and Sleepy John Estes.

Sure enough, a few weeks later, I received an offer from Mo to pay $300 for a record. That was all there was to it. My first record contract, with a label that had released a lot of the music I adored, the old folk and traditional pieces I'd been listening to since I was a child. Now I just needed to find a studio where I could record.

I signed my one-page contract with Folkways, and I felt it was only appropriate that I come to New York City to meet the great Mo (short for "Moses") Asch. He turned out to be really cordial, but in a tough-guy New Yorker sense. Despite his tough exterior, he had a grandfatherly demeanor. I admired him and what he had accomplished with the label. I'd be joining an artist family, and I felt certain that the label would look after me.

Mo told me that before Folkways could release my record, I needed to contract with a publishing business to secure my original compositions. I didn't have a manager, a lawyer, a publisher, or a booking agency at the time. I was just me. I was entirely on my own, taking my chances. I ended up signing a contract with Alpha Music, a tiny company recommended by Mo. He claimed that all of the musicians who signed with Folkways had publication contracts with Alpha. They had a brother-sister type of bond. That arrangement with Alpha would come back to haunt me in an almost comical way.

One of my father's best friends at Millsaps College in Jackson, Mississippi, was a man named Tom Royals, who went on to become a civil rights attorney in Jackson. Tom was one of these "guardian angels" who assisted me at crucial junctures in my career. When he found out about the Folkways offer, he called me and said, "I know a fellow who's an engineer at Malaco Studios here in Jackson." I assisted him in avoiding a narcotics charge, so he owes me a favor. Why don't I see if I can get you some studio time at Malaco and you can come here and record while staying at my house?"

Malaco was an iconic R&B and blues studio. There, musicians like as Bobby "Blue" Bland and Little Milton recorded. (Unfortunately, it was destroyed by a tornado in 2011.) I invited a guitarist from Houston named John Grimaudo, and we slept at Tom's place and cut the record in one afternoon. We recorded classic covers that I'd been doing for years. That's what was on my demo cassette, and I assumed that's what Folkways would prefer.

My Folkways CD came out later, in 1979, and I decided that the best thing I could do was relocate to New York City. I only stayed for around eight months since it was all I could tolerate. It was difficult to be there and broke. When I arrived in town, the wonderful folk culture I'd always read about—when Bob Dylan and Joan Baez were hanging out in coffeehouses and dreams were being made—was mostly dead, but some of the traditional venues remained open. There were also some fantastic up-and-coming singer-songwriters present. Suzanne Vega's performances blew the minds of everyone who had the opportunity to hear them. She was a lovely young lady with intriguing eyes and an air of mystery about her. She lured you into her sphere. Her approach to music was impressive: she had perfected the art of frugal and effective songwriting—clean and without frills, no vibrato.

I'd been to New York before, but never by myself. I was resolved not to be intimidated and to make it work, but there were always instances that could put your determination to the test. I once went to a laundromat and then went to buy coffee while my clothes were drying. When I returned, I discovered that someone had stolen my clothes from the dryer. But I persisted. I learned how to use the subway, frequently taking long excursions to the boroughs to play at venues like Flushing Local Coffeehouse. The journeys were frequently longer than the time I had to play, and I usually played for ten to fifteen dollars in mostly empty rooms.

I quickly found a sublet with a vocalist named Susan Osborn. We ran into each other on the street while she was busking. I was walking nearby and was lured to her wonderful voice. She sang with the Paul Winter Consort on a regular basis, and they occasionally performed at St. John the Divine Cathedral. We had a spiritual connection since she was a spiritual woman.

I eventually moved into an East Village flat with two other housemates on First Avenue and Second Street. I shared an apartment with a guy who was always crocheting and a singer-songwriter named Marie.

I became friends with Mike Porco, the owner of Gerde's Folk City, a little old Italian New Yorker who had taken an interest in my music. I signed up to be on the waiting list of performers in the event that a regular time slot on the Folk City stage became available. Mike would occasionally let me fill in for regulars who couldn't make it.

I strolled off the stage and into the throng toward the bar one night after finishing my show at Folk City. Mike approached me and said, "Loooo-cinda, I want you to meet a friend of mine."
"Of course," I said.

Then he turned around and pointed to a skinny, unnoticeable man seated on a barstool. We approached and Mike said, "This is Bobby...Bobby Dylan." I extended my hand without thinking, and then I realized what was going on and froze. My hero stood there in front of me, staring at me.

Dylan's management reached me two decades later about opening performances for him and Van Morrison on a tour they were undertaking together. I answered, "Hell yes, I'll do that." We played a couple months of performances together and I never got to speak with Bob or Van the entire time. Perhaps it's better that way. That lovely night is still fresh in my mind.

Chapter 10

Another guardian angel figure who appeared in my life was Hobart Taylor, who is still a close friend today. I met him in 1976, two years before signing with Folkways, while I was living in Houston and performing at Anderson Fair and other venues in Houston and Austin.

Hobart was originally from the Houston area. He'd recently graduated from Brown University in Rhode Island and returned home to work as a journalist for The Houston Chronicle. His family was one of the few black families in the South to maintain the land they farmed for generations.

Hobart enjoyed music and attended most of my performances at Anderson Fair. We were like the Three Musketeers, roaming around with another musician named Bill Priest. It was completely platonic. We did everything together, and Bill and I frequently performed back-to-back sets at different venues. Hobart later went to study with my father in Fayetteville for his MFA in writing, so we were all like family.

Hobart helped me and my music at difficult times. Years later, when my career took off, I was able to repay him in full.

Hobart had become good friends with another Brown student called David Hirshland, who was interested in pursuing a career in music management. For a few crucial years, he and Hobart developed a sort of partnership in guiding my career. Hobart offered to pay $25,000 to make a demo tape, which we would then use to try to land me a record deal with a major label.

Throughout the early 1980s, I lived with a man named Clyde Joseph Woodward III. I met him through the Houston music scene. Clyde was yet another of these poet-on-a-motorcycle types. He was born into a country club family, but he didn't want to be that type of guy. He was a huge man, and he was quite protective of me, which meant a lot to me at the time. He wasn't a poet in the traditional sense, but he enjoyed poetry and was an avid reader. He aspired to be a musician but never put in the necessary effort.

I penned these lines about Clyde in my song "Lake Charles," named after the small town in Louisiana, which appeared on my Car Wheels CD about a decade and a half after my relationship with him ended.

Clyde and I used to drive from Houston and Austin to New Orleans and everywhere in between. It was my first longer-term romance. Clyde was a lot of fun to be around, but he had another side to him that I honestly didn't notice or didn't want to see during our relationship. He was an alcoholic, and his marijuana addiction progressed into cocaine and other amphetamine addictions during our time together. He was in that death cycle, mixing the depressant alcohol with the amphetamines. Some of my pals later told me that he was also a drug dealer, but he managed to keep that mostly hidden from me. Clyde adored and worshiped me, and despite his imperfections, I felt his warmth even when he was fucking himself—and us—up.

I'm proud of a few tunes from the New York demos. I still have a master's degree. "Pancakes" and "Jazz Side of Life," for example, were recorded under a different title for my Ghosts of Highway 20 album in 2015. Those demonstrations, however, were in vain. David Hirshland and Brian Cullman worked hard to get them noticed by labels. We had talks and showcase performances, but nothing came of it. The outcomes were always the same. "We don't know what to do with this," executives at record labels would say. "It's both too country and too rock for country." For two decades, I was caught in between country and rock.

When I was doing research for this book, I asked David, Brian, and Hobart about this time period, and they all remembered Clyde having a negative, distracting impact on those meetings. He was attempting to defend me, to be my de facto manager, but he was just a clumsy bully to them. Brian even admitted to being terrified of Clyde. I was completely unaware of this scenario. Brian also stated that it was evident to him that Clyde was using a lot of cocaine, which caused his moods to be unstable. That didn't occur to me until much later.

When we were sleeping at a motel and the phone rang, I realized I had to quit the connection with Clyde. I snatched it up, and before I could say anything, a man on the other end of the line yelled, "Where's my money?" "Where the hell is my fucking money?" It turned out that the man had given Clyde a large amount of marijuana to sell and was searching for his money. "Fuck, they're going to come after us," I thought. We're criminals."

It took me a long time to reach this point. I'm an outlier in the music scene, a late bloomer. I believed in myself, worked extremely hard, and did not give up. My father and grandfather stood by their convictions, and I am the same girl who grew up under their influence. I've not changed.

After we finished the New York demos, Clyde and I returned to Texas, and I realized I needed to be somewhere else, not with him. It was difficult because a large part of me adored Clyde. He did everything he could. David Hirshland came to visit me in Austin some months after it became evident that the New York demos weren't getting me anywhere. He was based in San Francisco and was attempting to handle me from there. He informed me that if I stayed in Texas, I would only get so far. I was already thinking that, but it was intriguing to hear it from his point of view. I started planning my move to Los Angeles. And I had to call it quits with Clyde.

In the middle of 1984, I relocated to Los Angeles. Clyde's condition deteriorated over time, and in 1991 I received word that he was in the hospital dying of cirrhosis of the liver. I promptly boarded a plane at LAX bound for Texas. I wished to see Clyde before he died. When my plane touched down, I called the hospital and heard that Dad had died during my flight. Margaret Moser spent Clyde's final hours and days with him, playing him music he enjoyed and reading him articles on topics he enjoyed. "Lake Charles," my song about Clyde, has a refrain with these lines that remember those final hours with Margaret.

Chapter 11

Hobart and David assisted me in finding an apartment in Los Angeles' Silver Lake neighborhood. It was a $400-per-month duplex on the southeast corner of Glendale Boulevard and Loma Vista Place. I was in charge of the upstairs, while Mahalia was in charge of the downstairs. Over the next few years, the songs I wrote in that flat would become some of my most famous.

Even though I was enjoying my new L.A. residence, nothing ever came easy or quickly. I can't recall all the weird things I did in L.A. to support myself while doing as many gigs as I could. Hobart recently reminded me that I used to work at Tommy's Tacos, something I had completely forgotten about. I worked as a bus girl there. I remember working at Rockaway Records in Silver Lake and Moby Disc in Sherman Oaks, both excellent record stores.

Marty, a radical lefty hippie-biker, ran the cool Rockaway store. He declined to carry Steve Earle's album Guitar Town because one of the tracks made reference to a "Jap guitar." Marty was such a lefty that he wouldn't even carry a record that became Steve's breakout.

I also worked at Pecos Bill's Bar-B-Q stand and, I believe, Barnes & Noble, though it could have been another chain bookstore. In bookstores and record stores, I felt at ease. I had a unique job selling gourmet sausages at supermarkets. I used to put up a cart inside a store and sell these delicious sausages to customers. I prepared samples and served them on toothpicks. There were other tastes available, including apple and maple. That was my favorite job. Nobody troubled me while I earned $75 for the afternoon.

The phone rang one day while I was sitting in the kitchen of my Silver Lake condominium. It was my friend, music journalist John T. Davis, a native Texan. He informed John that he recognized one of my songs in the pornographic film All American Girls in Heat. This is when the old Alpha Music contract reared its head. I had no influence on those songs. I was on the verge of falling out of my chair onto the kitchen floor. I couldn't decide whether to laugh or cry. I hadn't read between the lines of the Alpha contract, and I didn't have access to an attorney at the time.

I informed my manager, who contacted my attorney, Rosemary Carroll. She called Alpha's CEO, Mike Nurko, who had nothing to say. Later, I went to see the movie.

One of the nice things about Los Angeles in the 1980s was how diverse the music scene was. I was free of Texas's singer-songwriter and cosmic cowboy scenes. Nobody in L.A. questioned or cared what genre you were in, not the club owners or the listeners. The record labels, as usual, were sluggish to accept what was going on underground.

This mixed-genre scene in Los Angeles is sometimes referred to as the Paisley Underground, which is another name I try to avoid. The Long Ryders were one of the bands who effectively portrayed this fusion of styles. They were an outstanding country rock punk band. I began opening performances for them in late 1984 or early 1985. A drunk man in the audience heckled me one night at Raji's. He'd yell between songs, "You need the Long Ryders, you couldn't do it on your own, you aren't anything without the Long Ryders." The guys in the Long Ryders didn't appreciate it, so there was a barroom brawl, and this heckler wound up in the hospital. An LAPD detective contacted to say that the man was going to file charges against the band members unless they let him open a few performances. He turned out to be a frustrated musician.
Greg Sowders, the drummer for the Long Ryders, and I started dating. We met at the Music Machine. I was performing at a benefit concert with Dave Alvin and others. Greg was a small, handsome guy with long hair, a cowboy hat, a great grin, and a glitter in his eyes who charmed his way into my life. He often said, "I'm your ace in the hole." He had a little of that bad boy in him as well.

Greg moved in with me at the Silver Lake duplex, and we eventually married. However, the relationship was not meant to stay. He was seven years younger than me, which is irrelevant. The primary issue was that we were both constantly working, and he was constantly on the road with the band, so we never had a chance to concentrate on our relationship. We divorced after only a year and a half of marriage. I still keep in touch with him and his second wife. They came to my wedding in 2009, when my husband, Tom, and I were married.

Even though our marriage did not endure, the time Greg and I spent together was immensely beneficial to my career. That's when I penned the songs for my 1988 self-titled Rough Trade Records album. Greg claims that I composed all of my best songs during emotionally and psychologically bad times for me, when I was unhappy and stressed, and when my obsessive-compulsive condition was at its peak. I don't recall it that way, but I'm sure his observations are correct. I believe that music was my therapy for dealing with many of the traumas I experienced as a child, beginning when I obtained my first guitar at the age of twelve and continuing to this day at the age of seventy. In general, I don't think having bipolar disorder is beneficial to my music or anything else in my life. To be honest, my erratic emotions have caused some problems for others at times, when people expect me to do this or that and I instead do something else. I've struggled with something resembling obsessive-compulsive disorder, which frequently manifests itself when I'm feeling melancholy. It's as though the OCD is a coping mechanism. As if there's something I'm meant to be doing, and instead of doing it, I'll opt to rearrange everything in my closets while people are waiting for me.

Several events occurred in Los Angeles that spurred me ahead. The first was that David and Hobart had done an excellent job of packaging and selling me to venues. In the fall of 1985, I was a part of a program called "Millions of Williams," which featured Victoria Williams and the Williams Brothers, nephews of the legendary singer Andy Williams. Then, for over a year, I had a residency at Al's Bar, a fantastic club in an abandoned hotel in downtown Los Angeles. For months, I played there once a week with David Mansfield on guitar and David Miner on bass. They were both members of T.Bone Burnett's Alpha Band. Mansfield was, of course, a member of Dylan's Rolling Thunder Revue, and he'd played on my New York tapes a few years before. He is currently residing in Los Angeles. Without a drummer, David, David, and I made an excellent trio. I wish we'd taped it.

In its listings, LA Weekly summarized Al's Bar perfectly: "The famous downtown bastion for bohemian barflies is again offering varied entertainment." Located in the heart of the city's developing loft district, this comfy hangout would make Edward Hopper and Charles Bukowski pleased, and it boasts one of the best jukeboxes in the city, with selections ranging from Hank Williams to Echo and the Bunnymen."

I adore the literary allusion to a writer I knew from my father's gatherings in Fayetteville. Al's Bar encapsulated what I was attempting. LA Weekly was also incredibly helpful, frequently promoting my shows. People were noticing what I was doing.

Another place that was very meaningful to me was Raji's. It was a unique Hollywood location. "If you crossed the Ramones with the Arabian Nights, you might get something close to this club," LA Weekly said. His sultanic majesty Dobbs provides cold beer and wine, delicious Mexican food, and constant rock & roll.``

A couple executives from Rounder Records in New York once went out to Los Angeles to see me perform at Raji's. I didn't yet have my own band, so members of the Long Ryders filled in for me. I had another show at Raji's around the same time with the musicians who would later become my full-time band—Gurf Morlix on guitar, John Ciambotti on bass, and Donald Lindley on drums. For the concert, the club gave us five one-dollar bills, so I could give each of the guys one and keep two.

Soon later, I had the much-needed break. Columbia Records gave me a thirty-five thousand dollar development deal. Ron Oberman summoned me to his office at Columbia in Beverly Hills and told me he admired and trusted me. He proposed that the money be used to cover living expenses for six months while I recorded a demo with a band. The label would listen to the tape and decide whether or not to offer me a full record deal.

I'd wake up in my Silver Lake duplex and write on the back balcony in the morning sun. Then, in the afternoon, while the sun was streaming in through the west-facing windows, I'd sit in the living room and compose songs. Then Gurf, John, Donald, and I would perform those tunes in nighttime shows.

I wrote "Changed the Locks" at Silver Lake at the time. It's a traditional blues song with lyrics about unrequited love, which I was familiar with. Those are the easiest songs to create, especially when you're young and going through a lot of changes in your relationships. The same goes with "Abandoned," which I wrote at Silver Lake. Neither of those songs is about a specific person, but rather about the dissolution of relationships in general.

"Crescent City " was also written there. That song has numerous documentary fragments from my life. Clyde has a link because he enjoyed Louisiana and New Orleans, as well as revealing, drinking, and dancing with pals. My brother, sister, and mother are all mentioned in the song. "Crescent City" is a short song full of autobiographical references to them.

"Side of the Road," one of my favorite songs from my career, was penned there. I was thinking a lot about how I had a propensity to lose myself in relationships. Many women will entirely surrender to guys and lose sight of who they are as individuals. I was also inspired by an Andrew Wyeth artwork I saw in a book a few years ago. It was a portrait of a depressed woman.

The song "Passionate Kisses" is about Greg. The Long Ryders were taking off, and he was constantly on the road throughout the United States and Europe. This was the first time I had spent time with someone who was always gone. I was usually the one that was always out or gone. Musically, the song owes a lot to Joan Armatrading. Both "Am I Too Blue" and "Big Red Sun Blues" are about Greg. Despite the fact that our relationship was structurally strained due to the fact that we were two full-time musicians attempting to make careers materialize, I tended to blame the problems on my personal despair or blues.

I started writing "I Just Wanted to See You So Bad" in 1979 or 1980, but I didn't finish it until I signed with Columbia. It's about Bruce Weigl, a poet I had a thing for. I was living in Houston at the time, and I had a job in Little Rock at the same time that Bruce had a poetry reading. I'm not sure how we actually met. Perhaps he knew my father through the poetry community. In any case, I was smitten right away. I went to his reading, and he went to my show. He had that rugged, good-looking poet character, like Sam Shepard—handsome, humorous, intelligent, and rough and tumble. The sensitive manly gentleman. Part of me wants to remain up all night talking about philosophy and art, while another part of me wants to be pulled into the bedroom. Another of these individuals who could do both was Bruce.

Bruce and I stayed in touch after Little Rock. Then one day, while I was at home in Houston, I received a phone call from him. He informed me he was in San Antonio for a writers' conference and asked if I wanted to spend the weekend with him. Of course, I said yes, stuffed some belongings into a suitcase, hopped in my Saab, and went to San Antonio. His meeting was held in a lovely Art Deco hotel downtown near the river. I had no idea what was going to happen when I drove to San Antonio. I was expecting us to have a lovely weekend love affair.

Of course, things did not end well. Bruce believed it was a good moment to tell me he was married and his wife was pregnant when I arrived. That's all right. However, my love for Bruce and the anticipation of our meeting in San Antonio inspired me to write a song that launched an album that altered my life.

"The Night's Too Long" was completed prior to the Columbia deal. It was written not long after I came to Los Angeles. I want to imagine that the song was inspired by the film Looking for Mr. Goodbar, but it was also about going out at night and seeing the same women over and over again.

These were the tunes I was working on for the demo. They were also the tunes I was performing in gigs at the time. Columbia hired Henry Lewy to create my demo. He was a celebrity. He'd produced all of Joni Mitchell's breakout albums, including Blue, and he'd also worked with Neil Young and Leonard Cohen on tracks. Henry enlisted the help of a number of well-known musicians to perform on my demo, including Garth Hudson from the Band, Terry Adams from NRBQ, and the famed New Orleans pianist Henry Butler. I was thrilled and eager to have these famous musicians perform my song, but in retrospect, we should have cut the demo with my usual band rather than this all-star group. Ron Oberman and his Columbia colleagues in L.A. listened to the ensuing tape and declined to offer me a full record deal. They claimed it was too rural for rock. They sent the tape to Columbia execs in Nashville, who rejected it because it was too rock for country.

Despite being incredibly deflated, I managed to muster the energy, with the assistance and confirmation of David and Hobart, to go through another round of meetings and showcases with labels, using the revised demo. Every single one of them turned me down. We tried them all, large and small, and they all passed on me, most of them for the second time.

"Changed the Locks" is still one of my most popular songs, and its structure is the same as it was back then. Tom Petty, one of my favorite songs and singers, covered it masterfully in 1996. That is certainly something to be proud of.

Chapter 12

One thing I've learnt through the years is that hard work will be repaid in some way. But I didn't know this in 1986, thus I was disappointed when I was rejected by every label after recording a significant demo.

The reality was that I was now thirty-three years old, which was considered old for a relatively unknown female singer at the time. It could still be ancient. I'd spent two years in L.A. playing every gig at any place that would take me, and for the majority of that time I was simultaneously working at energy-sucking day jobs to pay the bills, and now I was back at those jobs. I was fatigued and discouraged, but I persisted. I was still hopeful. Gurf, Donald, John, and I continued to perform concerts using the repertoire I had created. They, too, continued to believe.

Around that time, I recorded a song for the A Town South of Bakersfield compilation album. I collaborated with the engineer Dusty Wakeman, who would become a longtime friend, during that recording. Dusty introduced me to Pete Anderson, who was a major figure in L.A. at the time, having worked with and produced Dwight Yoakam. Pete appreciated my music and wanted to assist me in obtaining a record deal. He formed a band, and I recorded yet another demo with him, this time with only four songs.

I went back to selling sausages in supermarkets and working at a record store. The music industry's decision-makers were all men. So, in retrospect, I was pitching sausages on two distinct levels.

When I was sitting around the Silver Lake apartment, Greg was on the road with the Long Ryders, and nothing was happening in my career except the same shows around L.A., my phone rang, and it was a man named Robin Hurley from Rough Trade Records, the British punk label that had recently, unbeknownst to me, opened an office in San Francisco called Rough Trade America. Copies of my Columbia demo tape were circulating, and college and independent radio stations would occasionally play tracks from it. I'm not sure how Robin found out about it, but he got his hands on the

Columbia demo. He also discovered and like my Folkways release Happy Woman Blues. "We love your voice and your songs," he said. Do you want to collaborate with Rough Trade on a record?"

I almost tripped and fell on the floor. In my experience, it takes exceptional guts for an executive to say things as Robin did. There were no meetings, no showcases, no talks of this or that, no nonsense, just straight up saying we love this and want to create your record. "I'm in," I declared.

I've always liked to say that it took a British punk label to give me the opportunity to make a mainstream record. Something about that was just right. I later learnt that when Robin started working for Rough Trade America, his mission was to find vital and unknown American musicians who didn't fit into commercial bureaucrats' molds. Robin forwarded the Columbia demo to Geoff Travis, the overall head of Rough Trade in the United Kingdom. Geoff had worked with artists such as the Smiths and Aztec Camera. Robin didn't believe Geoff would enjoy my demo, but he loved it just as much as Robin.

For me, this was a no-brainer. Rough Trade was a fantastic, outlandish label that I needed to be a part of. They offered me a budget of $15,000 to make the record, which was less than what Hobart had given me for the New York demos. But none of that mattered to me. This was a true label with personality, vision, and courage.

Gurf was born in Buffalo but relocated to Texas when he was in his twenties, and when I first met him, he was playing with Blaze Foley. I liked him right away, but we didn't become serious collaborators until we were both living in Los Angeles. He was a skinny man with long dark hair parted down the middle, and he had a natural manner with the guitar that I admired.

The songs were ready because the band and I had played them so many times in gigs. We could go into the studio and play the songs just as we had done onstage. That's most likely how the punk bands on Rough Trade accomplished it. We'll do it, I reasoned. And so we did. In June 1988, we recorded the album at Dusty Wakeman's Mad Dog studio in Venice Beach. We just had a couple of weeks to complete the record. I believe we only did one song per day. It was a pretty natural approach, which I still favor now.

Later that year, in 1988, the record was released, and my life was forever transformed. I was prepared for it. I was 35 years old and had basically been performing music every day since I was twelve, while also doing day jobs to make ends meet. Rough Trade sent me all throughout Europe and the United States. It was the first time I could tell myself, "Wow, I'm doing this." I make a living by singing and performing music. It's effective." And I've been doing it ever since.

Chapter 13

All of the major labels that had previously turned me down were now approaching me and attempting to sign me. They wanted me right away, but I refused to sign with a major label. Fuck the major labels. I wanted to continue with Rough Trade because they were so encouraging when no one else was, and it seemed like a small family there. But I was already aware of their meager finances. Rough Trade records were only ordered in limited quantities by record stores. They lacked the promotional and distribution reach of a larger label.

Then I got this offer from RCA's Bob Buziak. The only reason I thought about it was because Bob was cool and had a good reputation. He had signed several brilliant, edgy artists, like the Cowboy Junkies and Treat Her Right, whose lead vocalist went on to form Morphine. I was dumb and naive enough to believe that Rough Trade and RCA could combine, that Rough Trade/RCA could exist. I chose to sign with RCA, which was a difficult decision that I eventually regretted. Rough Trade attempted to sue me for breach of contract, but my lawyer recognized that they had let the recording agreement expire, and I was free to go. I kept in touch with Robin Hurley, and when we released the 25th anniversary edition of that album, I asked him to write an essay for the sleeve notes, and he delivered.

Bob Buziak left RCA almost as soon as I signed with them for a comparable position at Elektra Records. I didn't blame Bob for leaving, and I eventually saw why: he was trapped in a suffocating corporate bureaucracy. So here I was, contractually bound to RCA, but without the entire reason I had considered joining with them in the first place—Bob. The replacement for Bob had recently transferred from Nashville. I don't recall his name, but everyone described him as "a numbers man."

I'll never forget what happened when Gurf, John, Donald, and I started working on the following album's production. Bennett

Kaufman, the label's A&R (artist and repertoire) representative, came to the practice room in L.A. to discuss possible producers for the album.

We started working on "Six Blocks Away" first because RCA wanted it to be the first single. We completed an initial mix of the song, which was submitted to RCA's New York offices for Dave Thoener to remix for radio. I'd never dealt with anything like this before. Because this was before digital recordings, they delivered the preliminary mix to New York on a hard-copy tape through FedEx or UPS or whatever. It felt as if something really important was being released and taken to an unknown location where people would interfere with it. This felt even more terrible than the guys peeking over our shoulders.

"Hey, I got the remixed track back from New York," Kaufman said one day from his office in Beverly Hills. Come on over to my office and we'll talk about it." So I drove over to Beverly Hills, where I was working on a huge attitude. When I arrived into Kaufman's office, he was listening to the tune and jumping up and down in his Gucci shoes, saying, "Isn't this great? It now sounds like a record. It sounds like a real record," as if it hadn't sounded like a real record before Thoener put his hands on it. "I fucking hate this," I exclaimed. "I hate it." Despite my warnings, they went ahead and released this remix as a single.

When it was my turn to speak in Austin, I recounted everything exactly as it had transpired at RCA. I was forthright. My manager, who was furious, called me the next day. He worked for one of the industry's most powerful promoters. "Congratulations, you were kicked off RCA," he added. He was disappointed, but I was overjoyed. I was liberated. I eventually signed with Bob Buziak once more, this time at Chameleon, a part of Elektra Records where he was now working.

"Little Angel, Little Brother," one of the songs I created during this time, is still one of my favorites, if not the best song I've ever written. It's a mournful tribute to my two-year-younger brother, Robert. It's a collection of photographs and impressions I have of my wonderful young brother, tinged with sadness. He read Shakespeare's whole canon and memorized much of it. He has the makings of a great musician. He was extremely gifted. After high school, he spent much of his time in New Orleans, where my mother lived, and he once performed a one-man musical performance under the stage name Rockin' Bob. He was an excellent pianist and singer. But there would be extended stretches when I had no idea where he was. When I was still married to Greg, the Long Ryders had a gig in New Orleans, and Greg spent some time looking for Robert without success. He could be found at my mother's place on occasion. He'd show up and play her piano for hours on end, staying for days, weeks, even months at a time. Then he'd go for a while and then return. Something had happened to him that I'm still not sure about. I can only speak to my own childhood traumas and battles; I'm not aware what Robert's struggles were.

I recall walking in from the street to see my mother in New Orleans at Christmas Time, and a person emerged in the hallway. Mama was dressed in her nightgown. I could smell the alcohol permeating her pores. She made a motion to me, as if she was communicating something. She forced a half-smile. I returned the wave. She wanted me to know she was present. Robert was working in the kitchen. He and I departed to go to a bar. We discussed music and other topics. We didn't talk about our mother's situation. We really didn't need to.

Today, Robert resides in Los Angeles with a friend, virtually as a recluse. We barely communicate. I'll send him emails every now and then, asking if he wants to meet up, but he rarely responds. I recently sent him a card that stated nothing but "I love you," and he simply replied, "I love you, too." His reaction seemed like the heavens had opened up to me. However, I wish I knew more about him. I wish we lived closer together.

Chameleon released Sweet Old World in 1992. "Hot Blood" is noteworthy because it was the first time I wrote directly about lust, which is something that women aren't allowed to do, despite the fact that the history of rock and roll could be told through guys composing songs about lust. "Hot Blood" was not inspired by anyone in particular. I envisioned a female persona for the song's point of view, however I'm sure there's a little of me in there somewhere.

I had moved to Nashville by this point. There were Steve Earle, Emmylou Harris, and Rosanne Cash living there at the time. John Prine was present. Griffith, Nanci. By that time, I knew several of these musicians personally. It felt like a safe haven for me. Greg and I had already broken up, so now was the time to make a move.

But I wasn't in the best of moods when I initially arrived in Nashville. I despised what had become of country music. They were irritated because I wanted to sing my song "Pineola." They complained that it was too dark. It wasn't "good morning music," they said. It didn't suit their image of traditional American morning music. But because it was the only song I wanted to perform on their show, I stuck to my guns. They eventually gave in, but it left a terrible taste in my mouth. It triggered my rebellious instincts. I had a feeling Nashville wasn't going to work out for me.

Later that year, something truly wonderful occurred. Mary Chapin Carpenter recorded "Passionate Kisses" and it got to the top of the charts, introducing my work to a whole new audience of popular music enthusiasts. That song earned me a Grammy nomination for Best Country Song. My reaction was conflicted. Of course, I was flattered and pleased, and I was grateful to Carpenter for providing me with this kind of opportunity, but I was also timid and afraid. The prospect of really attending the Grammy ceremony, for example, was terrifying. "What am I going to wear?" my mind raced. Will I come across well? "Are my teeth attractive enough?" I was examining myself under a microscope.

My journey to New York was completely planned. I had a flight booked, a hotel room reserved, and Rosanne set up an appointment at the clothing store, where they knew my measurements and had a selection of items ready for me to try on.

The truth is that I was both self-conscious and terrified. I was afraid I didn't fit in. It's a sensation I've been attempting to shake my entire life. It's a conundrum that I feel many artists have been attempting to answer for generations. It takes immense courage to produce the work in the first place, but the confidence required to go public is unconnected to the daring that generated the piece. That worry doesn't bother me as much as it used to, but it still comes up now and then.

Chapter 14

Sweet Old World provided me additional attention and chances, including offers to perform at events and festivals all around the world and to sing on other people's records. During that Sweet Old World tour, I got to know Roly Salley, who was in my band at the time. He was a long-time bassist in Chris Isaak's band and also played with John Prine. On the Sweet Old World tour, he played bass in my band. He was another of the amusing, bright, and intriguing men who came into my life and inspired numerous songs on my next album, Car Wheels on a Gravel Road.

Roly followed me tenaciously, and I was instantly charmed. We had an odd sexual chemistry and became very entangled with one other. "Joy" and "Still I Long for Your Kiss" are songs about Roly. When Roly began pursuing me, I was still dating another man named Lorne and was dedicated to him. Lorne came to town for the gigs one night when we were in New York City. As a result, we were all staying in the same hotel. I felt I needed to act like an adult and tell Lorne about my feelings for Roly. Lorne remained silent. He began taking up items in the hotel room—lamps, chairs, tables, and the television—and hurling them against the wall as hard as he could. I was afraid, sitting on the side of the bed. I was worried he'd hurt me, but he never did.

I eventually got out of the hotel room and down to the lobby, where I summoned my tour manager, who went up to Lorne's room to calm him down. My tour manager told me I may return to my accommodation a short time later. Lorne had bought a six-pack of Budweiser and was sitting on the bed sipping beer when I arrived. He was crying and bitching at me at the same time. We spoke about it all night, how this was the end of the relationship.

I said my goodbyes to Lorne, bless his heart, and climbed up the steps onto the tour bus, where I sat next to Roly. You can see what's coming now, but I couldn't. "I broke up with Lorne, so I'm free now," I said to Roly. "I'm all yours." He had an expression on his face that I had never seen before, as if he was astonished and terrified, as if he was thinking, "Oh my God, what the fuck?" At that moment, everything between us changed. "We have to get off this metal firecracker," he remarked, referring to the tour bus, "because everything is going to explode." He meant that we should wait until the trip was finished before continuing. That, of course, never happened. Our relationship took a nosedive when we got off the metal fireworks. He did not keep his word. But he managed to keep me hanging on for a while.

I was at a strawberry festival in Northern California shortly after the tour ended, and I was still hung up on him. The event organizers had placed me in one of these log cottages without a phone. In the parking lot, there was a phone booth. I stepped into the phone booth and dialed Roly, saying, "I'm sick and tired of this nonsense." "I'd like to know where I stand."

"I love you, but this relationship isn't on my agenda right now," he explained.

"Okay," I responded as I hung up the phone. I went to my room and sobbed uncontrollably. Later, I discovered that he was engaged with a number of women at the same time he was with me, some of whom were prominent musicians. I'm not going to name anyone. That relationship was over, but I got a fantastic song out of it that ended up on my Car Wheels album.

Chapter 15

I was seeking a new label after the Sweet Old World tour. Around 1995, Rick Rubin expressed interest in signing me to his American Recordings label. He was at the point in his career where he could be quite picky about who he worked with.

Rick's home was adorned with religious symbols. Rick played us the latest PJ Harvey record as an example of a direction he might see me going when we arrived. That was a fantastic idea. Rick could see I wanted to rock out a little harder. He had an effect on me that few others had.

The only issue was that Gurf didn't like the concept. Gurf began to perceive himself as my music director or co-collaborator as my popularity grew, much like a co-pilot or something. He wanted more and more control over the music, as well as more credit for it, and he refused to collaborate with another producer like Rick.

I was ready to try new things as a songwriter at the moment. Something was welling up inside of me, but I couldn't put it into words. The Rough Trade and Sweet Old World records had been successful, and I was now in a position to evolve and go forward, less concerned with finding a foothold and more eager to take steps up the artistic ladder. I was in my forties and no longer the girl working in retail.

I was staying in Nashville at one of those chain hotels that cater to long-term rentals, such as Stay at Home Suites or Extended Stay. That's where I wrote several of the songs for Car Wheels on a Gravel Road. I liked the concept of not having to make a large commitment, such as a lease or mortgage. It appeared to boost my inventiveness. There was a laundry room in the building and I had a pullout Murphy bed. The majority of the songs I created for the album are about my youth, my love life, or my job.

"Lake Charles," about Clyde, and "Drunken Angel," about the artist Blaze Foley, whom I had known and befriended while living in

Texas, were two of the first new songs I wrote. Both men were destroyed by their harmful habits.

"Lake Charles" was written in 1992 or 1993 while I was on the road for the Sweet Old World tour. Clyde died in 1991, and I'd had all these notions about him in my head for a long time. He was one of those individuals who had more talent than he realized. He was brilliant, humorous, and soulful, but he was also messed up and could be abusive. To me, not physically, but verbally. We had these horrible fights, one of which I recall him picking up a plate and smashing it against the wall.

I believe I wrote so many songs about Clyde because he was so difficult. He might be at ease in diverse worlds. He had this bizarre blend of refinement and intelligence, but he was also a lunatic. He could talk himself into anything. In such a sense, he was charming and astute. I couldn't dismiss him as if he didn't exist because he was an important part of my life and I loved him, God bless him, and he loved me.

I was thinking about my Silver Lake duplex flat when I penned "Right in Time." I had a mental image of this small kitchen with an antique stove and a woman pondering about her love interest. I began with the sentence "the way he moves is right in time" and worked my way up from there. While writing that song, I was thinking about the guitarist Bo Ramsey, whose performance I admired and on whom I had an unrequited crush."Right in Time" quickly evolved into something else. It is about a woman's yearnings and ambitions. In my brain, I was making a mini-movie.

"Car Wheels on a Gravel Road," the title song, came from a dream I had one night. The dream inspired the phrase "dogs barkin' in the yard." I started with that one line and then added a few more. Then I dozed off again, and when I awoke, I added a few more lines. This occurred on numerous evenings in a succession. As a result, the song evolved gradually rather than from a grand idea. That's why I didn't realize the child screaming in the backseat was myself.

"2 Kool 2 Be 4-Gotten" was inspired by a photograph in the photography book Juke Joint by Birney Imes, which I discovered in the Davis-Kidd bookstore in Green Hills, Nashville. I could spend hours shopping in that store. It was a two-story business with a small café on the ground floor. That's also when I discovered Shelby Lee Adams' book Appalachian Portraits. In Knoxville, I began composing "2 Kool" one morning. I was hungover as fuck on New Year's Day. Brian Waldschlager, a musician in a fantastic band named the Dirtclods, was my boyfriend at the time. They performed a mash-up of rock and hillbilly punk. I'd travelled over to Knoxville for a New Year's Eve performance. There was a large group of us there. We were all intoxicated and dancing, and I ended up kissing a girl on the dance floor as Brian and the band were performing onstage. Brian told me the next morning that I had embarrassed him the night before. "How?" I inquired. "By making out with that woman right in front of me and everybody," he explained. And I started composing "2 Kool" right away.

When I'm writing a song, I let my mind wander anywhere it wants. The process is mostly a stream of consciousness. I don't want to say I don't know how it happens, but it's nearly impossible to describe my songwriting process in words. I'm not always sure where the tunes come from, and I'm not always sure where they're headed. I put a lot of thought into my work and then let instinct determine the judgments.

I don't just sit down with a blank sheet of paper and begin from scratch. I keep all of these references and notes in a briefcase with me at all times, and I could utilize them at any time. So anything that was intended for one song may end up in another. Little fragments of information combine to form a song. This briefcase is still with me wherever I go.

I began writing "Concrete and Barbed Wire" with the fall of the Berlin Wall. It was intended to be ironic. Why aren't you able to knock down this wall? It's composed entirely of concrete and barbed wire. I imagined two lovers stranded on opposite sides of the wall, attempting to reunite. Of course, the wall is figurative rather than actual. I began with the line "dogs are at the gate" because I was thinking about Clyde at the time, his passion for Louisiana, and how he could shatter my heart yet had limits to his power. "Back in Algiers, my darlin' broke my heart, but he still can't seem to break down this wall." I'd been wanting to incorporate the term "Algiers" into a song for a while, and I finally found a way to do so in this one.

My song "Greenville" was inspired in 1978, when I was recording my first Folkways album in Jackson, Mississippi, and residing at Tom Royals' house. That October, I went to the Greenville Blues Festival and met the lonely Vietnam veteran with the guitar. I also ended up mixing some photographs from my acquaintance with a singer-songwriter named Eric Taylor, whom I met while performing at Anderson Fair in Houston. He drank a lot of alcohol, took some pills, turned on the stove, and passed out next to it. He didn't die because he neglected to close the kitchen windows and doors. I began writing a song about him, which I later included in "Greenville." Because the songs had the same tune and speed, it made sense to mix them.

Chapter 16

I went ahead and signed with Rick Rubin's label, but Gurf was to be a co-producer on the new record with me, not Rick. I began to suspect that Gurf's demands were impeding my progress. If he truly desired complete control over his music, I believed he should go out on his own. Rick approached me and asked, "Have you ever considered working with different musicians?" "Are you putting together a new band?" That thought scared the crap out of me at first. "Oh no," I exclaimed. "This is my group. I'm devoted to them." I was guarding the men. They had stood by me as I built my profession in Los Angeles.

Despite these reservations, we began recording the new album later in 1995 with the same band and Gurf as producer. We began out at Arlyn Studios in Austin, which was owned in part by Willie Nelson. Rick was unable to join us in the studio, so we would ship cassettes overnight to him in L.A. and then wait for his feedback on the tracks.

This setup was doomed from the start. The air was poisonous. Gurf didn't want to hear what Rick had to say, and I screwed up big time. Gurf and I were bound to have a nasty falling out—and we did. We agreed to take a pause from recording to let things settle. I returned to Nashville. Gurf and I went into Woodland Studios after our break to overdub some vocals on a few tunes that weren't working. "Jackson," a really sensitive, almost gospel-like acoustic hymn that required a lot of care, was one of them. It was also very significant to me because it is still one of my favorite songs to sing.

"Gurf, the track's not right," I said after a few minutes in the studio. It isn't working. Something else must be done." But he refused to listen. He was adamant that we were making progress.
"Do it again," he continued, "just do it again."
"No, I'm not doing it again," I stated emphatically. "It's not right." We kept bumping against each other. He returned to Austin, while I remained in Nashville and we had another break.

I was having these dumb flirtations with various men at the time. I recall this young writer who was maybe fifteen or twenty years my junior. During this time, Steve Earle approached me and requested me to sing on his song "You're Still Standing There" on his album I Feel Alright, which would be released the following year. I went to Ray Kennedy's studio to get my voice recorded. Ray had worked with Steve on almost everything he'd ever done. Ray's studio was crammed with vintage guitars and other vintage instruments he'd amassed over the years. He has a vintage manner of doing things, even though he is up to date on all new technology. Ray's production of Steve's song sounded fantastic with my vocal. I fell in love with Ray's sound after Steve gave me a CD of the rough mixes for his album. In my thoughts, alarm bells went off: this is it, this is how I want my record to sound.

We had preliminary mixes of all the songs that ended up on Car Wheels at this stage. Gurf assumed we were finished with the final mixes. But when I listened to our preliminary mixes alongside Ray's rough mixes for Steve's CD, the audio worlds were very different. Steve's album sounded far superior to mine in my opinion. I desired to enter Ray and Steve's sonic realm.

Unfortunately, the animosity between Gurf and me grew even more. Somehow, something had to give. It couldn't last. We made the decision to take another break. Gurf never returned, and I never asked him to.

Even with Gurf out of the picture, there was still a lot of pressure to finish the record, which created some tension. I am a very meticulous person who does not like to be rushed, and if I want to retake a vocal, I simply want to be able to redo a vocal. There were no questions.

I walked into Ray's studio one day and told Steve and Ray, "I want to redo my vocal on 'Lake Charles.'" "No, you don't have to do that," Steve said. When are you going to be able to trust someone, Lu?"

But I persisted, and Steve finally said, "Lu, it's just a record for God's sakes, come on, get over it."

"It's not just a record," I pointed out. He thought I was underestimating myself, that he knew better. To be fair, he thought I was smart and stated so, but he also said I was driving him insane. I ended up crying and sleeping in the fetal position in my vocal booth one night. I occasionally felt overwhelmed by pressure, and one of my fight-or-flight responses was to simply check out in whatever way I could.

"I'm done," Steve said when he arrived at the studio a few days later. That's all. I'm fucking booking a plane ticket to New Orleans and getting out of here. "I'm done." He didn't actually depart, but he got his point across. He stayed until we finished everything and then left to continue on the road.

But I believed there were a few more details that needed to be put to the record.

My bass player, John, knew Roy Bittan, the longstanding keyboard player in the E Street Band, and we contacted Roy for the finishing touches. When Roy wasn't on the road with Springsteen, he was doing his own engineering and production work in Los Angeles, and he told John he'd be pleased to work with us. We flew to Los Angeles to work with Roy at Rumbo Studios in Canoga Park.

Despite the turmoil with Gurf and the tension between myself and Steve, the several studios and towns, and the mounting recording expenditures, we finally finished the album. I believed we'd finally made it to the finish line. Then, out of nowhere, a huge new impediment appeared. Rick Rubin's label, American, was in the process of changing distribution companies, so he opted to hold Car Wheels until the new distribution agreement was finalized. Rick stood guard over the CD for two years.

Five years had passed since Sweet Old World, and I still hadn't released a new record. Rumors began to circulate about how difficult I was to work with. A lengthy, heinous feature story on me appeared in The New York Times Magazine, fueling those allegations. The author made me out to be a control freak. His piece was titled "Lucinda Williams Is in Pain."

Throughout this time, I performed as many gigs as I could in order to earn money and have fun. Finally, my manager, Frank Callari, who had known Rick from their early days in New York, decided to try something different. Rick's spiritual side was new to him, and Frank was interested in it as well. Frank contacted Rick at home one night and said, "Dude, you gotta do this, man." It's a spiritual phenomenon. Look into your third eye, Rick, and tell me you don't see that Lu's record needs to be put out there."

Rosemary Carroll, my attorney for nearly my whole career and still today, had given a copy of the song to her husband, Danny Goldberg, who was the head of Mercury Records, and Danny loved it. He was so taken with it that he persuaded Mercury's upper management to send a check for $450,000 to purchase my contract from Rick at American. I didn't find out about this deal till many years afterwards. All I knew was that there was a good label eager to release the record sooner than Rick expected.

We had to make selections on the packaging and cover art when the record went into production at Mercury, which was another drama. The Mercury PR staff were hesitant at first about my request to utilize Shelby Lee Adams' images, but eventually agreed. Adams was born in eastern Kentucky but lived in Boston and taught at one of the city's institutions. He traveled to Nashville with one aide to assist with equipment transportation. Mercury brought many public relations representatives from New York to the shoot.

I didn't want the PR images in the book; I wanted photos of Shelby Adams and Birney Imes. I was having trouble deciding which of their images to use, and I knew I would have to make a significant push with the PR guys to get what I wanted. I was sitting in my Nashville kitchen when my attorney, Rosemary, called and said, "Lucinda, I don't care if this record comes out in a brown paper bag." You must choose now which art to include on the record." That's the end of the narrative. I chose the Imes photograph for the front cover and the Adams photograph for the rear cover. Mercury, happily, agreed to follow my wishes.

Car Wheels was published six years after Sweet Old World, in 1998. It received a Grammy for Best Contemporary Folk Album and remains my best-selling album to this day.

My relationship with Gurf is a sad component of the Car Wheels story that continues to this day. It happened twenty-five years ago, and he still refuses to speak to me. I'm not sure why, and he won't tell anyone, not even mutual friends. He still believes that his Car Wheels mixes are superior to what was released, and he says so openly.

Tom and I went to see Gurf perform at a little bar in Los Angeles a few years ago. This occurred not long after the death of our old band's bassist, John Ciambotti. Our drummer, Donald Lindley, had died a decade before, leaving Gurf and me as the only remaining members of the band. Both deaths were unexpected. I reasoned that it was finally time to mend things with Gurf. Furthermore, Tom had never met him. I was hoping we'd be able to clear the air. I made an effort to attend his event because I believed it could mean something to him. Instead, he brushed us off. The next day, he emailed me and asked, "Please stay out of my life." Tom was enraged, and the mere mention of Gurf still riles him up. It has wounded my heart for a long time, but I can understand that we will never be able to mend fences, even if I still wonder, "How can someone be that bitter after all these years?"

Chapter 17

When Car Wheels was being prepped for distribution, Danny Goldberg came up with the idea of having filmmaker Paul Schrader create a video or short film based on "Right in Time." I typically refused to produce videos for any of my songs, but Schrader had made some renowned films and written scripts with Martin Scorsese for films like Raging Bull and Taxi Driver and all that.

The expression "sex, drugs, and rock and roll" implies that rock and roll performers are the only ones that get out of hand and behave in problematic ways. But, in my perspective, musicians are a cleaner bunch than the aforementioned literary types and the ones I later encountered in Hollywood. Over the years, I've spent a lot of time with male musicians, and the majority of them keep things professional.

Schrader planned to put the film in a 1940s antiques business managed by a husband and wife, with me playing the wife. The husband would then be called away to fight in Europe, leaving the woman alone. The duo would be seen dancing around the antiques shop the night before he left.

When I wrote "Right in Time," I imagined a noirish black-and-white video of a woman alone in her apartment, with lots of oblique shots of her ending up in the bedroom, taking off her bracelets and earrings, lying back on the bed, and doing her thing, though you wouldn't be able to see it on camera, just oblique glimpses. I had no intention of working with Schrader. He was just another guy imposing his vision on a female artist. Without a video, Car Wheels performed admirably.

My career took a different turn with the release of Car Wheels. I signed a contract for a new six-album agreement with Lost Highway, a division of Mercury led by Luke Lewis, who was always a pleasure to work with, as well as extremely intelligent and sincere. Basically, I had to create an album every year for the next six years. My entire life structure shifted. I had more money, two tour vans, and more responsibilities. For the first time in my life, I had this steady thing. I was in my late forties, and I was prepared. Prior to this, my employment had been inconsistent, and my life had been chaotic. Things were happening consistently now, and I could see further down the road. I don't recall feeling pressed to release six new albums. It was thrilling.

By the end of the 1990s, Nashville had evolved into a party town. Ryan Adams moved to town at that time. It was a major issue for him to go to Nashville because young musicians like him normally settled in Los Angeles or New York. He was about twenty-five years old and the leader of the well-known country music band Whiskeytown. This was before he released any solo material. Frank Callari was handling both Ryan and me at the time.

A year or so after Car Wheels was out, Frank took me to see Ryan at 12th and Porter, a popular Nashville hangout with a restaurant on one side and a small performance venue on the other. Ryan was alone, just him and his guitar and harmonica, dressed in jeans, a T-shirt, and a denim jacket, like he usually does. When he started playing, I was utterly taken aback.

Ryan liked Frank, and I liked Frank, so it was easy for us to hang out together. We were all at a bar one night, including Frank and Ryan and two girls who worked for Frank. When I was younger, I would order beer with tequila shots. I preferred wine, but there was no wine worth drinking at a Nashville pub at the time. Ryan introduced me to vodka tonics, and it was the beginning of the end for me.

What transpired between Ryan and myself was nearly insignificant because it wasn't a true love affair. It was only a friendly flirtation. Ryan and I both enjoyed flirting. Flirting is vastly underappreciated. Ryan was twenty-one years my junior, but that didn't matter.

We connected musically and intellectually on many levels; there was instant appreciation and understanding. But, because of our age gap, the chance of a meaningful relationship was non-existent, so no one was thinking about it. It was unthinkable. However, that impossibility also allows things to happen.

Ryan leaned over to me one night after a few vodka tonics, when we were laughing and having a fantastic time, and said, "We need to go somewhere and make out." So we went outside the pub to the courtyard and started rolling about and kissing. I bit his lip at one point. That's just how I am in high-stress circumstances, and plenty of guys appreciate it. Then I bit his lip one more. He drew back and warned, "Don't bite." "Sorry," I said, and he stood up, walked away, and left. I didn't hear from him for several months.

Chapter 18

When I was younger, I used to listen to other musicians and say to myself, "I don't want everything to sound the same." "I want to be eclectic and use a variety of styles." I aspired to be someone like Bob Dylan or Neil Young, who could do whatever they pleased. That is not something that many women have. Everyone tries to confine them in some sort of preset box. Bob Dylan and Neil Young can make albums in a variety of styles, but it's still them. That's what I wanted to be since I was a child. Tom, my husband, recently told me that he read somewhere that said, "All of Lucinda's records are different, but at the center they always retain Lucinda." It's the highest compliment I've ever received.

With my next album, I wanted to go in a different direction. I'd won a Grammy for Car Wheels, so I expected a similar follow-up, but I wanted to make something different. Fans become emotionally engaged with the narrative songs on Car Wheels, such as "Drunken Angel," "Lake Charles," and "Greenville," I believe because they recognize themselves in the characters. But I wanted to move away from narrative songs and focus more on how the overall thing sounded.

When I began working on "Are You Down," which has fewer lyrics than my previous songs, I recall thinking, "Wow, I like this, but can I really make records with songs like this?" When I learned I could, it was a watershed moment for me.

To be honest, one thing that may have pushed me in this path was that once Car Wheels came out, everyone started humping me in with Americana or alt-country, which, as I previously stated, I despise. They are extremely restrictive. I knew they were trying to be complimentary, but it still hurt me, so I told myself, "I'm going to do something different." That's just my personality.

When I finished writing the songs for Essence, I submitted them to my father, as I always did, because he'd have tiny suggestions for changing a word here and there, and who's kidding who, I was also

looking for his approval, which is something I've had to go through in therapy. I was hesitant to deliver him these new songs because they were so unique, with less words overall. He contacted me after reading the lyrics and remarked, "Honey, this is the closest you've come to pure poetry yet."
"Really?" I queried.
"You graduated, yes."

I recall him using the term "graduated," and it prompted me to reflect on earlier instances in my career where I had graduated and gone on to larger, better, and more autonomous things. After that, I didn't feel compelled to keep sending my songs to my father.

Dylan's album Time Out of Mind, produced by Daniel Lanois, came out while I was working on the songs for Essence, and I adored it. It was stunning lyrically, musically, and sonically. That's the kind of sound and feel I wanted for my next album. I was also listening to Sade's Lovers Rock album, which was released in 2000. It had a mood about it that was carried through the album's music, which ranged from reggae and dub to rock, folk, soul, and R&B.

Some people said I was daring to attempt something new, but I was truly terrified at the time. I wasn't sure if it would work, and I had a major new contract with Lost Highway. I already had "Blue" and "Bus to Baton Rouge," which were old, old, old songs, and I thought I'd put them on the record to appease the people who wanted the narrative stuff, but I realized I could record them in a new way, and the rest of the record would be all about the groove.
I recorded a demo of the tracks with guitarist Bo Ramsey by myself. I sent the sample to Lost Highway, and Luke Lewis went crazy. "This is so good," he continued, "we could release the record just like this." As a result, we agreed that Bo would co-produce the album with me. I was overjoyed.

Bo and my manager, Frank Callari, recommended a variety of players, and we ended up with a fantastic band for the recordings. Dylan's bassist, Tony Garnier, and guitarist Charlie Sexton joined us, as did famed drummer Jim Keltner, and Bo and Ryan Adams also played guitar. On the record, Jim Lauderdale sang harmony vocals, as he had done on Car Wheels.

Before we began recording, Bo, Frank, and I went to see engineer Jim Dickinson, who had worked on the Replacements' breakout album, Pleased to Meet You. He was living in a trailer with his wife in Coldwater, Mississippi, near Memphis. They had purchased a large tract of land and placed a trailer on it with the aim of constructing a lovely house. But it had been a few years and they had yet to break ground. On the premises, there was also a recording studio. He hadn't heard my records and didn't seem to know who I was. So we said our goodbyes and thanked him for his time.

Bo described a man named Tom Tucker who owned a studio in Minneapolis called Master Mix. In that studio, Bo had worked on a number of records with Greg Brown. Tom had also done a lot of engineering for Prince at his studio. I quickly agreed because I admired and respected Bo. So we arranged for the entire band to gather there, and I sent the duo demo that Bo and I had recorded in Nashville to all of the musicians so they could study the songs.

In around ten days, we completed the basic tracks for Essence. We were on a tight timetable after we were in Minneapolis because Jim Keltner had to go back out on the tour with Neil Young, Charlie Sexton, and Tony Garnier had to go back out with Dylan. As a result, after those folks went, there was some fiddling to be done, a few faults that needed to be addressed without the musicians still present.

Tom Tucker had discovered a young man who was an expert at Pro Tools, an early computer software used by many audio and video editors. This was my first time with Pro Tools, and this child was fantastic.

That album is fantastic. Today, many people approach me and tell me that Essence is their favorite of my records. I try not to choose favorites, but I understand when someone does.

I stayed alone in Minneapolis. I switched from a historic hotel to an Extended Stay hotel, where I had a suite with a kitchen. It was the first time I'd ever spent Christmas by myself. I'd heard that one shouldn't spend Christmas alone, but I figured it wouldn't bother me because it's just another day.

My father and stepmother went to Rome for Christmas when I was about twenty-one, so I was in New Orleans with my mother and brother. Mom was doing drugs and drinking one day, and I had to leave the apartment. On Christmas Eve, I was of legal drinking age and strolled into a bar. It was the first time I'd ever been alone in a pub. I felt emancipated in an odd way since I didn't have to deal with my family. My father and stepmother were away, and my mother had checked out for the day and night. I recall thinking to myself, "Wow, this is kind of cool in an odd sort of way." It was the first time I realized how much I appreciated being alone. And it's been true for the majority of my life.

While Tom and I were finalizing Essence, Bo Ramsey was in and out of Minneapolis, assisting us as needed. He could simply travel back and forth because he lived in adjacent Iowa. I'd had a long-standing infatuation with Bo and decided to try to make things happen between us during one of his visits. I went out and bought candles and incense for my hotel room, as well as some delicious food and wine, and I invited him to my room to "work on the album." I had given considerable attention to what I would dress and what I would say in my attempt to seduce him.

When Bo entered my room, candles and incense were lit. Sade was playing on the boombox. My attempts at seduction went completely over his head, or beside his head, or whatever. He showed little interest in reciprocating my amorous efforts and kept the evening solely focused on the record and our professions.

Bo and I ran into each other a few years later, and I reminded him that I had attempted to have sex with him. He exclaimed, "What? Why didn't you inform me you were doing that? I would have been delighted to help."

I blew my opportunity. Bo was married to Greg Brown's daughter Pieta at this point. But at the very least, we'd recorded a great record.

Chapter 19

I hadn't seen Ryan Adams since the night he walked away in Nashville a few years before, but he came up while I was in Minneapolis recording Essence. Ryan came to town to play some gigs while Frank Callari was still managing both of us. We all stayed in the same motel.

Ryan was in the lobby when I first noticed him, looking untidy and unruly in his jeans, T-shirt, and denim jacket, his hair a dirty mess. He was seated there, engrossed in section A of The New York Times, the page spread out in front of him. Ryan saw me, put the paper down, and instantly began flirting with me again.

I had resolved to have him say "I'm sorry" for abandoning me that night at the Nashville bar and never phoning or responding to any of my informal overtures delivered through Frank. Ryan was such a good kid, as if he could never do anything wrong, and I was going to make him say "I'm sorry."

We parted ways after three days in Minneapolis and were barely in touch after that. That's all there was to it. We never had sexual relations. But our meetings did inspire a song. "Those Three Days," which I authored, was released on World Without Tears in 2003. It's not a literal account of what happened. In fact, I'm still baffled by what happened between us. People have informed me that they relate to it, possibly because it is so difficult to understand attraction.

I made it to the Hotel San José, where my band and traveling companions were staying. I passed out on the couch in my suite, still dressed. I awoke with a terrible hangover, thinking to myself, "Fuck, I've got to meet Annie Leibovitz for this photo shoot, and I'm fucking hungover and look awful." As a result, I took a shower. I washed my hair, which is something I never do before a photo shoot. That was a lesson I learnt years ago: never wash your hair before a photoshoot. Leave it soiled.

Annie arrived at my San José suite at the scheduled hour. She took one glance at me and immediately responded, "Oh..." Then there was a long pause, which was a little odd. I had just gotten out of the shower, and my clothes were on but no makeup or anything. "I'd love to photograph you right now the way you are," she added.

I'd never worked with a photographer who had me stand there and grin even when I didn't want to. She didn't mind if I smiled or not. She knew how I felt and didn't press me into a different pose or position. It made no sense to me at the moment. But then I saw the photos and thought, "Oh my God, this is why she's so good."
Most of the photographers I work with can sense whether a shot will be cool or not while it is being shot. You can't tell anything about Annie. She informed me that every time she shoots someone, the subject says, "This is the worst shoot I've ever had." Nothing interesting will come of this." They can't believe it when they see the images.

Chapter 20

We started seeing some strange stuff from the stage once Essence was released. I suppose I'd created a kind of cult following among some of my fans. There were reports that I was doing strong narcotics like heroin. I'm not sure where they started. I believe it had something to do with the subject matter of some of my songs. Then there are a few references to heroin on World Without Tears. But I've never experimented with hard drugs.

I had a concert in Denver around that time. It was probably the first time I'd ever performed at altitude, and I wasn't aware of the repercussions. We were staying at a Kimpton Hotel, and there was an Aveda salon with all of these treatments in the lobby. I had this amazing massage, but you don't want to do that before a show; you want to do it after. Following the massage, I ordered room service and drank a couple of glasses of wine, like I usually do before concerts. But this time, the combination of the massage's relaxation, the altitude, and the wine left me wobbly onstage. A few people who attended the show commented about it on the internet, questioning if I was high. Not long after that, I was conducting an interview with a journalist, who asked me, "When did you get out of rehab?"
"What?" I inquired.
"You weren't in drug rehab, were you?"
"You've got the wrong person," I pointed out.

I came the closest to doing heavy drugs when I was living in Austin in 1974 or 1975. I was living in a house with roommates when I decided to try amphetamines, which I liked. They were these tiny pills known as white crosses. When I was smoking marijuana, I'd have one of them every now and again because I enjoyed the way it tasted. But I didn't keep it up for long. For one thing, you needed money to buy hard drugs, and I didn't have any.

When I got some extra cash, I decided to try crystal meth. There was this guy in Austin who sold pure crystal meth. With his long hair and large eyes that were usually wide open, he reminded me of

Ginger Baker. He was a speed demon, but everyone liked him since he was always smiling and having a good time. I contacted him, and he showed up at our house with this massive fucking bag of crystal meth, which terrified me. I recall thinking that the doses weren't manageable and that I didn't know how much you were meant to take. I informed him that I had changed my mind. I've always felt like I had an angel on one shoulder and the devil on the other. This time, the little angel triumphed. I stopped using heavy drugs once and for all. Over the years, I've primarily stuck to wine and occasionally mixed beverages.

Granted, I've had a few too many drinks, just like my father and his writer buddies when they threw those literary parties at our house in Fayetteville. Even today, one of my favorite pastimes is getting together with a few pals for a few beers and a meal.

Chapter 21

Essence was released in June 2001, while World Without Tears followed less than two years later, in April 2003. We didn't stop touring during those years. On the road, I wrote World Without Tears. Those tunes just flowed out of me. My life at the time was chaotic and stressful, but in a wonderful manner. My career was taking off, and new opportunities were opening up.

I relocated from Nashville to Los Angeles. It was another of my erratic, nomadic movements. When I wasn't touring, I was staying at the Safari Inn in Burbank, a beautiful 1950s motel. It had been meticulously restored throughout the years.

I turned fifty a few months before the publishing of World Without Tears. The majority of the songs on that album were inspired by men with whom I had brief but powerful relationships.

One of them was a bartender called Billy Mercer, whom I met near the conclusion of my time in Nashville at 12th and Porter, the same venue where I first heard Ryan Adams perform. He'd played bass in Ryan's band before, but he wasn't a professional musician.

I was drinking at 12th and Porter the night Joey Ramone died, and Billy was bartending. His shift ended after a time, and a few of us headed to another bar called the Slow Bar. Everyone was getting hammered and crying over Joey Ramone's death. We were dancing around and singing Ramones songs. Billy and I ended up making out like ferocious creatures in the Slow Bar's toilet. When we departed, I went to his house with him.

Billy and I were completely incompatible—he was nineteen years younger and in a very different situation than me. My time with Billy was the inspiration for the songs "Fruits of My Labor," "Righteously," "Overtime," "Sweet Side," and "People Talkin'." However, the relationship was not progressing in a personal or intimate sense. It just died away.

My song "Ventura" was composed in the midst of the Billy and Ryan era, although it isn't really about them. Twenty years after the release of World Without Tears, I was working with the renowned jazz saxophonist Charles Lloyd, who told me that "Ventura" was one of his favorite songs of mine. He knew everything about me, which was flattering, but the comment about "Ventura" meant a lot to me because Charles is from Memphis but has lived in Santa Barbara for many years, so he had a southern and Southern California mix similar to mine.

I wrote "Real Live Bleeding Fingers and Broken Guitar Strings" after spending time with the Replacements' lead vocalist, Paul Westerberg. It was yet another brief affair. He had clearly been staring at me from afar for years. In my early days in Los Angeles, when I was doing shows at places like Al's Bar, Raji's, or the Troubadour, the Replacements would be on the same weekend bill as me. I saw them live at the Palace in Los Angeles, and they were loud, intoxicated, and great. A few years later, someone sent me Paul's solo album 14 Songs, and I fell in love with it and his other solo recordings.

Paul and I eventually became acquainted, and I saw him a few times when he visited L.A. We spoke on the phone, and I attended his gigs. He got shitfaced drunk at one of his gigs and wanted me to sit in on one of his songs with him. He was always messed up.

My connection with Paul didn't continue long because he was so unpredictable, such a hound dog. He was a shambles. But he possessed the same attributes that drew me in: knowledge and talent. He was telling me about his wife and their son at one point, and I told him, "Look, you need to go see a therapist to sort all this stuff out." That irritated him. He was completely enraged. I said, "See ya later." It was all over.

"World Without Tears" is merely a remark about life and its difficulties. That's a song I usually sing anytime there's a catastrophe in the country, which seems to happen every week these days.

I walked into the studio with my band, Doug Pettibone on guitars, Taras Prodaniuk on bass, and Jim Christie on drums, with the tunes in hand. Doug and Jim both grew up on the coast, around Oxnard or Ventura, and were avid surfers. Taras had been raised in the Valley. These guys were true L.A. boys, capable of playing nearly any genre of music.

When we started looking for record producers, I was still thinking in terms of Dylan's Time Out of Mind sound. That record was produced by an engineer named Mark Howard, who previously worked with Daniel Lanois on Emmylou Harris' Wrecking Ball and many other projects. Many of Mark's records with Lanois were recorded in ancient houses in New Orleans that had been converted into studios. Mark had recently established a studio in an old house in Silver Lake, so we approached him and he agreed to collaborate with us.

Mark's new studio was in an 18-thousand-square-foot hilltop house. It was erected in the 1920s by a socialite who acquired a large sum of money from the oil industry. She was married to a silent-film actor, and rumor has it that they hosted lavish parties with visitors such as Buster Keaton and Charlie Chaplin.

When the album was released, Ann Powers wrote a terrific review in which she characterized the situation very well in her first remarks.

Looking back, I notice that Car Wheels, Essence, and World Without Tears constitute a sort of trilogy, which I didn't intend. My career had been about taking tiny leaps over time, and in those three records, released over a five-year period, everything was uncorked. We recorded World Without Tears in a similar manner to how we recorded Rough Trade. We went into the Paramour and just blasted the songs. We wanted it to be alive, fresh, and nasty. In some respects, the trilogy represents three distinct approaches to composing music about sex, love, and the status of the world—or my world.

Chapter 22

I was 51 years old, and my life and career had never been more intense. I was either traveling with my band or staying at the Safari Inn.

We had a sold-out event in Charlotte, North Carolina on March 8, 2004. The theater was rocking when we arrived backstage. A phone call came into the theater's headquarters just as we were about to go onstage. I'm not sure who phoned me. My mum was no longer alive. The presenter walked out onstage and informed the audience of what had occurred, and I was later told that the audience received the news well. There were no boos or other such noises. We also had to cancel a lot of other shows.

She was 73 years old when she died, and although having lung problems, her death was unexpected. She had remained in New Orleans until I supported her in moving into an assisted living home in Fayetteville, which I had paid for.

She had remarried several years previously to a good man, an exploration geologist. He'd died before she did, and she hadn't left a will. As the oldest child, I was given legal power of attorney.

When my mother's brother Cecil arrived, it was an absolute nightmare for me, one of the worst experiences of my life. My mother did not want a large sum of money to be spent on her funeral. She stated that she did not want a casket. She desired to be cremated and her ashes placed in an urn.

Uncle Cecil and his wife drove from their home in Sulphur, Louisiana, to Fayetteville when they learned of my mother's new life. I was at the funeral home, looking for an urn, when they came in. Uncle Cecil insisted on a casket and a conventional burial, and that my mother be buried beside her parents in Monroe, Louisiana. That is the polar opposite of what my mother would have desired.

The situation was hopeless. I was overcome with emotion and felt duped into agreeing to a traditional funeral. The entire process ended up costing me $11,000, which I agreed to pay. When my brother and sister came, the chaos intensified, and I couldn't see through it. I was overly emotional.

So much of Mom's treatment was about coming to grips with the harm done to her by her parents and family, which she had struggled with her entire life. It was too much for me to bear knowing they were transporting her body to Monroe to be buried among her parents. I was unable to attend the funeral. I eventually got through it by creating a song about it. "Fancy Funeral" appeared on my 2007 album.

Because my mother was mentally sick, my father was my anchor. But he, too, had issues. My family was not permitted to discuss difficulties aloud. Everything was kept within. I was never able to express my displeasure or annoyance to anyone. In retrospect, I wonder whether it would have been better if you could yell and scream, "Fuck you!" and slam the door and walk away. Then it's all over the next day, and you start afresh.

My therapist refers to "frozen moments," which occur when a traumatic incident or experience is stuck in your psyche and causes physical symptoms ranging from acid reflux to migraine headaches to whatever else. One of those frozen moments for her was when my mother locked me in the closet when I was three years old because she couldn't deal with regular three-year-old stuff. "Keep holding her until you feel like she becomes one with you," she kept urging. In other words, the three-year-old girl and the 68-year-old woman are not distinct. We are the same individual. You have to step in and take hold of the young girl and tell her everything is going to be okay, everything is going to be okay, everything is going to be okay. I felt so much better after I became one with the tiny girl. It was a guided visualization state, and I informed my therapist that I didn't want my three-year-old self to vanish, to which she replied, "She won't vanish." She'll join you, and you'll make her safe and comfortable." It is all about love. You adore that three-year-old version of yourself. You adore her, you embrace her, and she resides within you. You love her with all your heart and give her everything you have.

I can also tell that my mother was affected by this emotional condition. It had to be the result of her father and older brothers' terrible sexual abuse. My mother's narrative enrages me more and more as I grow older. Her father hid behind the pulpit at church. He crouched behind the Bible. He took cover behind the crucifix. It's awful and repulsive to think of him standing up there speaking to a congregation. He should have been imprisoned. My stomach turns just thinking about sitting in his lap as a child. My grandfather, who was meant to protect and cherish me. He destroyed my mother's life. She was never given an opportunity.

I wrote a song about this disturbing internal struggle that people experience after being mistreated as children for my 2003 album, World Without Tears. When I penned this song, I had a certain ex boyfriend in mind. He was a person I met while living in Nashville. He worked as a bartender and occasionally as a bass musician. However, he could have been anyone. Anyone could be the subject of the song. The song is called "Sweet Side."

This tendency of mine reached a nadir, or violent low point, in 2004, when I returned to Los Angeles. It was around the time that my mum died. I performed at a winery in California, a lovely location someplace along the coast. I observed this attractive and friendly member of the crew team. He was like a puppy dog—can I take him home, Mama?

Matthew Greeson was his name. He was living in a sober living residence in Los Angeles at the time. He'd been there for a while and had progressed to the point where he could work outside of the treatment center. He appeared to be in good health and joyful.

I'd been around a lot of people—both men and women—who drank a lot and partied hard, but almost all of them were just trying to unwind and have fun. They laughed more as they drank more. They were drinking to have a good time. For the most part, they are celebrant, joyful kinds. They wanted to forget about their concerns for a few hours without causing any more problems for themselves or others.

Matthew was a unique individual. He began imbibing here and there after we had been dating for a time. He claimed to have it under control, and I believed him, or at least pretended to believe him. He was initially really sweet to me, and I adored him for it. But he quickly began to drink more and became aggressive about trivial matters.

Matthew and I spent one night in Memphis at the historic Peabody hotel. It is a large downtown hotel that has been present since the early 1900s. There is a large lobby with a fountain in the center, and mallard ducks have lived in the hotel for decades. They wander around the hotel and swim in the fountain.

I'm not sure why we were in Memphis, but I recall being fatigued and wanting to sleep. Matthew stated that he was heading to the bar below to have a drink. When he returned to the room, he was a completely different guy. I was tired and wanted to sleep, but he had other plans for me. He was looking for some hard sex with me. I let him remove my clothes. We were both completely naked. We began wrestling. It started as playful, but he gradually became more violent. He shoved me down onto the bed and choked me with his arm across my chest. He became increasingly rough. I was unable to move. I started to feel terrified. It was the first time I'd been afraid around him. I was afraid he was going to kill me. I thought I was going to die in the Peabody Hotel.

I mustered the courage to crawl away from him. I went over to get the phone. He lunged on me and yanked the phone from my grasp. I dashed to the door and made it out into the hallway. I was still naked as a buck. Matthew stormed out into the hallway, naked, and the door closed behind him, locking us out without a key. A hotel security guard soon arrived. He unlocked our door and welcomed us back into our room. He then turned and went away. Back in our room, we both breathed a sigh of relief.

We made it back to Los Angeles, to my Burbank apartment. Matthew claimed to me that he was using heroin but that he had it under control, which was clearly not the case. I began to realize that a piece or two was missing at some time, but I never said anything. Then I discovered one of my Grammys wasn't there. I assumed Matthew was stealing these items and reselling them to fund his drug habit. When I confronted Matthew about it, he erupted in a frenzy. The rest of the narrative is presented in my song "Wakin' Up" from my 2020 album, Good Souls Better Angels.

I called a friend that night. She handed me a copy of the AA manual, hoping it would help me decide what to do. I eventually returned Matthew to rehab. He realized he had to leave.

I relocated from my flat to the Safari Inn on my own. The Safari Inn was always my happy place, where I felt safe and at ease.

Chapter 23

At the Safari Inn, I penned the majority of the songs on my next two albums, West (2007) and Little Honey (2008). Many of those songs, particularly those in the West, are about me dealing with my emotions following my mother's death in some way. I also got by by doing as many performances as I could with Doug, Jim, and Taras, and we recorded a live album, Live at the Fillmore, in 2005.

With the success of World Without Tears and my growing chances, Luke Lewis at Lost Highway gave me a budget of $500,000 for my next album. I spent some time at the Radio Recorders studio in Hollywood, where Frank Sinatra had made many of his records, and made demos of twenty-four songs I'd composed at the Safari Inn.

In 2005, I also met my husband. I was at the notorious Whisky a Go Go in Hollywood one night to witness Hank Williams III, Hank Williams' grandson, who was blending punk and country in a new way. Damien had begun working on Shilah's hair when he excused himself for a second to meet his final appointment of the day, who was just walking through the door. When I looked up, I saw a tall and lean man with a big smile and dazzling blue eyes. Damien was the one who introduced us. His name was Tom Overby, and he said Bonnie Butler from Minneapolis was a mutual acquaintance of ours. He had recently relocated to Los Angeles from Minneapolis, where he had worked as Best Buy's music buyer. He'd secured a position at Fontana, a Universal record company, in Los Angeles.

Shilah and I had made plans to see a friend of ours, Susan Mitchell, sing a block away at the Hotel Cafe later that night, but we had some time before that, so we were headed to the Velvet Margarita for a drink. Tom joined us, and we drank some tequila—the Velvet Margarita is a popular Hollywood Mexican restaurant with velvet Elvises and Day of the Dead folk art. We went to the Hotel Cafe after a few tequilas and tortilla chips. After a while, I was feeling the tequila and realized I shouldn't drive home, so Tom offered to bring me back to the Safari Inn. I was completely smitten.

I encouraged Tom to come over to Radio Recorders after he left his office at Universal one night soon after we met to listen to my new tunes. Tom had attentively listened to all of my records before we met.

A few days later, Tom asked if I wanted to see Bruce Springsteen at the Pantages Theatre in Hollywood. It was the Devils & Dust Tour, and Springsteen was performing in smaller venues without his band. Tom said he could obtain tickets, but I replied, wait on, let me phone Frank Callari, and I did. We soon had tickets and backstage passes.

Bruce's performance was fantastic, and we went backstage afterwards. Jim Carrey approached me and raved about my music. We were introduced to Sam Moore of the famed Sam & Dave. T-Bone Burnett and his wife, Callie, and my old friend Jesse Malin, the vocalist in the legendary New York punk band D Generation, were among others I knew back then. When Bruce approached me and asked, "Hey, Lu, how ya doin'?" I was a little overwhelmed and had problems getting the words out, but I think I said something good because Bruce came over to me and Tom a few minutes later, after the crowd had thinned out, and invited us to dinner. We dined at Kate Mantilini's popular West Hollywood restaurant. It was Bruce, T-Bone and Callie, Jesse, U2's Edge and his wife, and me and Tom, a man I'd only known for a few weeks. It was thrilling, but also gorgeous and unearthly. Bruce kept attempting to talk to me, and I struggled at first, but I ultimately got there. All night, I kept asking myself, "Do you call the Edge "the Edge" in person or just "Edge," and does he have a street name? What does his wife refer to him as? The truth is that they were wonderful individuals, and I should not have been so worried. Bruce eventually got up and said he had to leave, but everyone was invited to stay and the money was paid.

We went to see Jason Molina and his band Magnolia Electric Co. at a dive in Echo Park on our third date. Tom introduced me to Molina's music, and I got obsessed with his albums. One day, I'd like to cover some of his songs. I recall Tom and I discussing album sales or personal economics that night, and he stated, "I'm good with numbers," which I thought was really cool. He also had the perfect amount of bling. I'd never met a man like him before.

On our first "date," we went to Radio Recorders to listen to my new tunes. Our second date was with Bruce and his friends. Then there was the Jason Molina concert. Not a bad beginning to what would become a wonderful and long-lasting marriage.

Tom established himself as a forceful new figure in my life. He wasn't one of those down-and-out poet-bad-boy-on-a-bike types who couldn't keep it together. He was quite intelligent. He also has the capacity to see that when I'm in a terrible mood, it's just a bad mood and not a problem that needs to be confronted, questioned, or avoided.

Chapter 24

Tom was on the tour bus with me in 2006. We were in Los Angeles, while the bus was in Nashville. It was a brief tour, with only me and Doug Pettibone on guitars and my father delivering a few poems.

"You want to go shopping for diamonds?" Tom asked me on the bus. That's how he put it. Tom claims that I made the statement, not him. He claims I asked, "When are you going to get me a diamond?" That's not how I recall it. Today, we joke about it.

The following show after Nashville was in Minneapolis two days later. Tom mentioned a terrific jewelry store he knew in Omaha, which was right on the route to Minneapolis. We rode the bus to Omaha and spent the night in the parking lot next to the jewelry store so we could make a decision the next day when the store opened.

I wanted to make the decision because I adored Tom, but I was also overwhelmed. I was terrified. I struggled to get dressed to go shopping. It took several hours.

We finally went inside twenty minutes before the business closed. There were numerous alternatives. I knew I didn't want a ring with a large, protruding diamond. I desired one with diamonds put within the band. The store had a "don't touch anything" vibe to it. Everyone seemed to be staring at me. "Make a decision, lady, make a decision."

I made a choice. We had gotten married. We boarded the bus and went to Minneapolis, the next tour destination.

Not long after that, Tom suggested, "Let's get married onstage," which I thought was a fantastic idea. Then we agreed to do it at First Avenue, a well-known Minneapolis bar where I had previously performed. It felt like a decent place to do it because

Tom is from there. When I told my father about our plan, he remarked, "That's perfect." Onstage, Hank Williams married."

It took us a few years to work First Avenue into our tour schedule. We finally tied the knot on September 18, 2009: 9-18-9. In numerology terms, it is one of my life-path numbers. I have a tendency to be New Agey, which stems from my time working in health food stores. The month is nine. One plus eight equals nine. The year was 2009.

We'd invited roughly half of the crowd, who had flown into town for the play and wedding. The other half had no idea they'd be witnessing a wedding. Some of my fans may have heard stories about it.

The band performed a standard performance before we began the encore with the wedding. My father presided over the event and read his poem "The Caterpillar," which was written about me.

My father also penned our wedding vows, which included the following line: "I love you for all the things I do not yet know."

We played "Happy" by the Rolling Stones after the wedding. Tom picked up a guitar and joined in with us.

We got back on the bus after our wedding and continued the tour. We did not go on a honeymoon. Our honeymoon was spent on a tour bus, which is now a place where we feel completely at ease together.

A year and a half before our wedding, Tom and I purchased a home in Studio City. We still live in that house, albeit we now divide our time between Los Angeles and Nashville.

Jordan, my stepmother, wrote me a letter sometime in 2010 in which she explained that my father had been diagnosed with Alzheimer's disease. Later that year, Tom and I went to see my father and stepmother in Fayetteville for the Christmas holidays. We were alone in the sunroom off the main room with my father.

Jordan was probably sleeping upstairs. We'd had a typical evening of drinking wine, talking, and listening to music. When we were present, my father was still able to keep it together. But then he said something to us that hit me like a ton of bricks. He informed us that his illness had deteriorated to the point that he could no longer write poetry or read it publicly in public. It was the saddest thing he could say to me. "Honey, I can't write anymore." It was the equivalent of stating he couldn't see or speak anymore.

I obtained a yellow legal pad that night and wrote him a long note, which I put on the kitchen table for him to read in the morning. I informed him that even though he couldn't write poetry anymore, he was still a poet.

He informed me the next morning that the note had moved him. He gave me a hug and thanked me. He also commented on how well worded the note was. The teacher is always right.

My father would gradually lose the rest of himself over the next four years. He was put into an assisted living memory care unit in late 2014, and he died on January 1, 2015.

EPILOGUE

Tom became my manager a few years after we married, and as I stated in the liner notes to my album West, he altered my life for the better. West was released on February 13, 2007, and I was supposed to do the biggest show of my career three weeks later. I sold out New York City's Radio City Music Hall in two days after tickets went on sale. I'd played several large festivals, but this was the largest arena I'd ever sold out as a headliner, with roughly 6,000 seats. It was also the biggest event by any artist on Lost Highway Records, so several executives flew in for the occasion. It was a watershed moment for everyone concerned. Tom and I were sitting outside in front of the bar next to our hotel a couple of nights before the play when I suddenly recalled that the street corner half a block away, at Fifty-fourth Street and Seventh Avenue, had been a significant site in my life.

"This is so incredibly strange," I exclaimed to Tom.

"What?"

"You won't believe it, but that corner is one of the ones I used to play for change when I lived here briefly in 1979." I lived in Brooklyn long before everyone else did. I'd ride the train to this area several times a week and play with tips to put in my guitar case."

"Are you kidding me?"

"Nope," I replied. "That's the location. It now feels like a dream."

Made in the USA
Middletown, DE
08 August 2023